# WAYNE WEIBLE

Author of the International Bestseller *MEDJUGORJE: THE MESSAGE*

*Medjugorje*

# THE LAST
# APPARITION

*How It Will Change the World*

*"Truly, I tell you, many men longed to see what you see, and did not see it..."*

## Testimonials for *The Last Apparition*

"What an incredible book about the love of the Blessed Mother for her children. My dear friend Wayne has captured that love in the pages of *The Last Apparition*. I pray that everyone will read this book and accept the great blessing bestowed on us by allowing the Mother of God to come to us in apparition."

—**Immaculee Ilibagiza,**
**author of** *Led By Faith* **and** *Our Lady of Kibeho.*

"No one is a closer or more insightful observer of the incredible events surrounding Medjugorje than Wayne Weible. He has caused countless people to visit and feel the transformation of this amazing place; and who in his book *The Last Apparition* grants us both a feel for what the future holds as well as the inspirational touch of the Blessed Mother."

—**Michael Brown,**
**author of** *Final Hour* **and numerous books;**
**founder of** *Spiritdaily.com.*

"*The Last Apparition* takes you back to those crucial days in June of 1981 and leads you through the years--all the while inviting you deeper into the mystery of God's presence. Wayne brings you into the lives of the visionaries, their families, and the priests. You climb the hill, you sit in a jail cell, and you kneel within inches of an apparition. You feel hope, anguish, love and peace as a village, a people, a church, *a world*. And you know--the best is yet to come! Simply put...the Mother of God uses Wayne Weible."

—**Michael Ripple, author of** *A Lost Shepherd.*

"The historical sweep of this engaging book makes it one of Wayne Weible's best yet. From the first intimate words Mary spoke to the Medjugorje visionaries to an insightful depiction of what may await us in the Medjugorje secrets, Wayne Weible artfully spans three decades of heavenly visitations. Rich in information, power, and grace, *Medjugorje: The Last Apparition* never grows dry in painting a colorful picture of the Blessed Mother's final call to help save her children. Comprehensive and convincing, this book is a passionate call to the world to rouse from its spiritual slumber. Keep it in your home or carry it with you to prayerfully share with others. There is no time to waste. The world must take Medjugorje seriously, for nothing less is at stake than the future of humanity."

—**Christine Watkins, MTS, LCSW,**
**author of** *Full of Grace: Miraculous Stories of Healing and Conversion through Mary's Intercession* **and** *The Illumination of All Souls: Stories and Prophecies of the Warning.*

*Medjugorje*

# THE LAST
# APPARITION

*How It Will Change the World*

WAYNE WEIBLE

New Hope Press
Hiawassee, Georgia

*The Last Apparition*
First Printing January 2013
Copyright 2012 by Wayne Weible
ISBN 978-0-9820407-9-9
Library of Congress Control Number: 2012950966

Printed by:
New Hope Press
Hiawassee, Georgia

www: newhopepresspub.com
newhopepress@windstream.net
Published in the United States of America

Cover design: Janice Walker
Cover Painting by Janis Horn.

**The painting of the Blessed Virgin Mary with the child Jesus is a rendition of the original "Madonna and Child on Flaming Orb" fresco on the wall of the Church of the Visitation, in Ein Kerem, Israel. It is also titled "Woman Clothed with the Sun." The date of origination and the artist is unknown.**

## Other books by Wayne Weible

*Medjugorje: The Message*
(also on audio read by author)

*Letters From Medjugorje*

*Medjugorje: The Mission*

*Final Harvest Updated*

*A Child Shall Lead Them*

*Are The Medjugorje Apparitions Authentic?*
(Co-authored with Dr. Mark Miravalle)

*The Medjugorje Prayer Book*

*The Medjugorje Fasting Book*

All of Wayne Weible's books are also in electronic format.

## ACKNOWLEDGEMENTS

The messages from the Blessed Virgin Mary were given to the visionaries in the past three decades at Medjugorje. They are verified from a variety of qualified sources, the most important of which has been by personal contacts and interviews with the visionaries, priests, and others involved.

The messages come under strict theological scrutiny by the Roman Catholic priests of the Franciscan Order stationed at the parish of Saint James Church in Medjugorje. They do so to assure each message is in total compliance with Holy Scripture and the doctrines of the Catholic Church. If any message, event, or activity originating in the apparitions were not in conformity, the Catholic Church would condemn the site immediately. After nearly 32 years, no such condemnation has occurred.

The wording and grammar of the messages are subject to the variance of translation from the Croatian language into English. No attempt is made to grammatically correct or alter any part of the messages in order to allow them to retain their original flavor. Virtually all of them are recorded just as they were received. They appear in bold italic type throughout the book; any emphasis added to them by the author is noted.

The author acknowledges that the final determination of the authenticity of the apparitions at Medjugorje rests with the Roman Catholic Church and submits entirely to its formal conclusion. Given the thorough investigations conducted in past years by theological, scientific, and medical experts—in addition to the abundant spiritual good fruits—they are accepted as authentic by the author until final judgment is rendered and are addressed as such in this book.

All scriptural references are from the New Revised Standard Version (NRSV) of the Bible. They appear in boldface type.

# Personal Acknowledgements

An author does not write a book alone. There are numerous people to thank for their special assistance, support and professional contributions. At the top of the list is a native of Medjugorje, Draga Vidovic, whom I have known for more than 25 years. She was actively involved from the beginning of the apparitions and shared in many of the experiences with the visionaries. Draga has authored a book titled *Salvation of Mankind*, which gives valuable first-hand perspectives by someone who was right there when it started. She has allowed me to use intricate detail of the early days of the apparitions from her book. I am grateful to Draga for her insight, information and confirmation.

I could not have written this book without the direct input from the visionaries, priests and villagers of Medjugorje through interviews and personal encounters as a friend and as a journalist.

There are family members, associates and friends who have given assistance and support. The list starts with the love, encouragement and critiques of my wife Judith, as well as her exemplary skill at editing. To all our friends and associates who were kind enough to read the manuscript and offer critiques, a grateful thank you.

A very special thank you to Pat O Mara, a great friend and promoter of the messages. He has generously supported all of my efforts, attempting to get me into every place possible to speak on the messages.

Of course, I must include my hardworking and loyal staff of Mary Maddox, Betty Cooper and Katie Davenport. It is their mission as much as it is mine to spread the messages.

To all of you, I am deeply grateful.

—Wayne Weible

# CONTENTS

| | | |
|---|---|---|
| i. | Introduction: Repent! | 1 |
| 1. | The miracle | 5 |
| 2. | Heaven's messenger | 13 |
| 3. | Hope for the world | 19 |
| 4. | On a warm day in June | 27 |
| 5. | Critical first days | 37 |
| 6. | Persecution | 53 |
| 7. | Opposition from within | 63 |
| 8. | Slavko, the lead shepherd | 81 |
| 9. | Jozo and the other shepherds | 97 |
| 10. | A special role for Mirjana | 107 |
| 11. | The other messengers | 123 |
| 12. | Jelena and Mariana: a new dimension | 143 |
| 13. | Colleen's miraculous healings | 153 |
| 14. | Her words to the world | 161 |
| 15. | Related apparitions | 177 |
| 16. | Who could make these things up? | 195 |
| 17. | The secrets | 203 |
| 18. | The Last Apparition: How it will change the world | 219 |
| ii. | Epilogue: But for the grace of God… | 231 |
| iii. | Bibliography | 234 |

Dedicated to the memory of
Slavko Barbaric, OFM
for his efforts in keeping the focus of Medjugorje
on its goal of salvation for the children of God.

*I have come to call the world to conversion for the last time.*
*Afterwards, I will not come in apparition any more on this earth ...*

> "The people who sat in darkness have seen a great light, and for those who sat in the region and shadow of death light has dawned." From that time Jesus began to preach, saying, "Repent, for the kingdom of heaven is at hand."
>
> —Matthew 4:16-17.

## INTRODUCTION: REPENT!

MYRTLE BEACH, South Carolina was a beautiful little beach town when I moved there in 1975. It was modestly popular on a national scale because of its pristine white sand beaches. Due to an escalating number of good public golf courses, it was also developing a fast-growing reputation as one of the golf capitals of the country. Mostly, it was a popular family-friendly vacation resort.

The family-friendly tag slowly began to erode with the introduction of more golf courses and an expansion of businesses catering to the golfers. The new businesses included bars, nightclubs and several so-called "gentlemen's clubs" featuring topless women as dancers and servers. Soon, such clubs dominated the area; soon, Myrtle Beach was no longer a family-friendly beach town.

A large indoor mall, the first to be built within the city, was part of the expansion and was welcomed by the residents. Its food court, located in the rear of the mall with its own entrance of huge glass doors and windows, became a favorite lunch destination for many business people, including me. It was the perfect place with a nice view to enjoy a quiet lunch and recover from the stress of daily business life.

One day while lunching in the food court, I was startled by a commotion near the entrance. I turned to see two teenagers no more than 18 years of age struggling through the glass doors with a large wooden cross. Everyone stopped lunch to watch.

Glancing around furtively, knowing the security people would be there at any moment, the young man righted the cross and took a stance next to it with the girl on the other side. In a quavering voice filled with a mixture of fear and determination he cried out, "Repent! Repent! Accept Jesus Christ as your Lord and Savior!"

For several seconds, there was not a sound to be heard in the food court. The young man repeated his message—this time with more force. Suddenly, the security people were there and swiftly hustled the two teenagers out of the doors with their cross. A tittering sound grew to a small roar as people reacted; a few were angry, some were embarrassed. Others laughed and made light of it. I sat there momentarily touched, realizing the courage it took for the youth to accomplish their witness.

The incident in the food court took place at a time before I learned about the apparitions of the Blessed Virgin Mary at Medjugorje. It was a period when I was not attending church at all, more wrapped up in my businesses than worrying about the fate of my soul. Like many other business people, I was glad with the growth of the area even if it meant accepting such an undesirable element with it. I rationalized, what difference did it make as long as it meant making more money?

Nevertheless, the message delivered by the young man that day in the food court stayed with me. It touched me and made me uncomfortable. I never forgot it.

Several years later, learning about the apparitions at Medjugorje became the impetus for my spiritual conversion. Somewhere along the way, I realized that the message given by the Blessed Virgin Mary at Medjugorje was the same as the one uttered by the brave young man in the food court that day: Repent! Repent! Accept Jesus Christ as your Lord and Savior!

The definition of the word "repent" is to show remorse, to be sorry for and to change direction for the better. That is what the teens were asking of the people in the food court that day. They were addressing negative changes taking place in our community, changes, which were not conducive with the faith of the people. It was a direct challenge to those who professed belief in God.

The messages of the Blessed Virgin Mary at Medjugorje are asking the same thing the young teens asked through their demonstration of faith. Her words challenge us to take a close look at life today and see it as it is. When we respond with blunt honesty, we cannot help but repent. We cannot help but put God back in the first place in our life.

Just as the reaction of the crowd in the food court that day was mixed, so, too, is that of those who learn of the grace of Medjugorje. Some laugh, some sneer. Many ignore its call or simply do not believe it. Others realize the courage it takes to listen, to accept and then to change. My hope is that the reader will see it that way and join those who respond to the call of repentance—for it is the heart of the message being given at Medjugorje.

**—Wayne Weible**

## CHAPTER I: THE MIRACLE

A GREAT spiritual miracle is happening daily in a remote mountain village in the European country of Bosnia-Hercegovina. It will soon change the world forever. Amazingly, a vast majority of the world's population knows little or nothing about it. If you are among those, you are about to discover one of the greatest of graces given by God.

The Miracle has been the stimulus for thousands of supernatural physical and spiritual healings. It has changed lives dramatically. Dire warnings have been issued about what will happen to our world if we do not listen and react. Yet, it has been overlooked, downplayed and ignored. One can only wonder how that is possible when it will have an unprecedented impact on every living being

Sadly, there exists a general apathy toward faith in God throughout the world today. Ignoring anything regarding spiritual faith and the supernatural is symptomatic of a humanist world led by a secular news and informational media. The attitude of the fourth estate is usually to ignore or belittle such claims, a position far from the objectivity that is supposed to be the landmark of journalism at all levels. No one worries about what is to come on such a grand spiritual scale. We are far too busy enjoying our tech-driven modern life to worry about our souls.

The "Great Miracle" is the ongoing daily supernatural apparition of the Blessed Virgin Mary, human mother of Jesus Christ, to six Croatian teens in a hard-to-reach obscure mountain village named Medjugorje. To date, more than 50 million people have made the difficult pilgrimage trek to the village. Its popularity as a spiritual pilgrim site has grown by quantum leaps. Once quiet little Medjugorje is now the second most visited Marian site in the world. The list of such famous Marian locations includes Guadalupe in Mexico, La Salette and Lourdes in France, Fatima in Portugal and Knock in Ireland.

Adding to the drama, the Blessed Virgin Mary has made it clear through her early messages that her appearance at Medjugorje will be the *last time she will be sent to earth in apparition.* There will never be another from the Mother of God on earth. She quickly adds, it will no longer be necessary.

The end of this incomprehensible grace of supernatural apparitions in Medjugorje is presumably close. When it occurs, it will be *the* conclusion not only of the apparitions at Medjugorje, but also of *all* presently active Marian apparitions. Surprisingly, there are many. The last apparition will be followed by the long awaited and often prophesized spiritual and physical purification of the world, which will be followed by the promised reign of the peace of Jesus Christ. Planet Earth and those *still alive* will never be the same.

If this gift of grace is authentic—and 31-plus years of good spiritual fruits confirms that it is—it is reasonable to state that the supernatural apparitions of the Blessed Virgin Mary in the little village of Medjugorje is the *most important event* happening in the world today. It directly affects you, me and every living human being.

Marian apparitions are not new. They have been an integral part of early Christian church history and tradition since its founding by Jesus Christ more than 2,000 years ago. Even before the earliest apparition of the Mother of Jesus, the original apparition arguably was the Transfiguration. According to Holy Scripture, Jesus, surrounded with an unearthly light, is suddenly seen by his disciples Peter, James and John in deep conversation with like entities of Moses and Elijah.[1]

Roman Catholic Church tradition claims the first apparition of the Blessed Virgin Mary actually occurred while she was still living on earth. It took place at what was then a small village in Spain called Zaragoza[2] around the year 40 AD. She appeared to James, the disciple of Jesus, to encourage him during a low point in his quest to spread the new Gospel message of his beloved leader. It marked the beginning of literally thousands of Marian apparitions over the centuries. Ironically, they always seem to occur at a time of crisis in a region, country or the entire world. The times we live in now definitely qualifies as a worldwide time of crisis.

The Medjugorje apparitions are composed of two distinct parts. First, there is the active daily appearance of the Blessed Virgin to the visionaries; second, the commencement and fulfillment of ten special prophecies for the future of the world given to each seer over the

---

1 **Matthew 17:1-3:** Six days later, Jesus took with him Peter and James and his brother John and led them up a high mountain, by themselves. ²And he was transfigured before them, and his face shone like the sun, and his clothes became dazzling white. ³Suddenly there appeared to them Moses and Elijah, talking with him.

2 Also called Saragossa; today, a large modern city in Spain.

length of their participation in the daily apparitions. The prophecies are the most critical element of the apparitions. They will begin only when she ceases actively appearing to the last visionary or visionaries. They will then occur one by one with a brief amount of time in between each. According to the Blessed Virgin through her early messages to the visionaries, the implementation and fulfillment of the secrets are what will forever change the world.

Belief that the conclusion of the active apparitions at Medjugorje could be near is based on years of personal investigation and involvement. That does not mean it can be predicted by me or anyone else within days, weeks, months or years per se. However, they have occurred far longer than any past Roman Catholic Church-recorded daily apparition of the Virgin Mary. More importantly, as of this writing only three of the six visionaries are still having the daily apparition. Lastly, her messages now more than at any time since its beginning, are a blunt call to urgent action. They contain stringent warnings to the unbelievers, the lukewarm in faith and the secularists of the world. She refers to these groups as "those who have not yet found the love of God".

The Medjugorje apparitions are not just a "Catholic thing" because the Blessed Virgin Mary is the messenger. I have learned through years of personal involvement in Medjugorje that most non-Catholics think of the Virgin Mary as simply Catholic—as in Roman Catholic. I personally believed that until discovering and becoming involved in Medjugorje. It is clear through Holy Scripture that her spiritual motherhood is for everyone, as you will see in the following chapter. It is confirmed through her messages to us given through the six visionaries. The definition of the word catholic is "universal." Thus, the messages are directed at every living human being—even those with no faith.

The same is true with the focus of the book. A primary intent is to bring non-Catholics and non-believers into an awareness of this special grace from God before it is too late.

The stark reality of present-day world conditions brings into sharp focus why the apparitions are occurring for so long a period. It does not require deep thought or investigation to realize that from a moral point of view, we are living in the worst of times. Wars rage on everywhere fueled by greed, lust for power and religious extremism. Many people no longer believe in the reality of God—or in the reality of Satan and the existence of hell. Many "believers" have watered down faith by basing it more on social issues rather than the commandments of God. In short, there is a growing apathy in belief in God among the majority of the world's population. This has led to a general global malaise of morality.

The greatest indicator of present-day moral decline is the proliferation of abortion of the unborn child. The womb should be the safest place possible for life. Yet, abortion is universally accepted as a way and a right of women for contraception and convenience. Those who accept or favor abortion often see the fetus, a living being in formation, as just a clump of cells and not an actual, unborn child. They do this despite clear scientific evidence that the "clump of cells" is a living being with a beating heart as early as 18 days after conception. It hides under the premise that it is a woman's reproductive right and freedom of choice. There is no consideration for the rights of the unborn child.

The rejection of the God-given gift of life makes abortion the most horrendous of all present-day wars having more casualties than all past wars in modern history combined. The deterioration of moral law is clearly evident in the acceptance of abortion as the civil law of the land in just about every nation, making its practice a legal choice and not a breaking of one of the laws of God.[3] I can think of no other act of rejection of God and acceptance of evil, which stands out so clearly as this glaring evidence. It is clearly a possible explanation as to why the Virgin Mary has come daily for so many years to the little village.

For more than 26 years, I have been immersed in all aspects of the apparitions, including constant scrutiny of the messages given from the first day to the present. Much time, professional and personal, has been spent with the visionaries and others directly involved, through formal interviews and casual conversations. I have written eight books about Medjugorje and traveled millions of miles across the globe lecturing on the specific message of the apparitions. It is a mission, and its purpose is to attempt to make people aware of this greatest of spiritual graces, which allows Mary to be the messenger, teacher and spiritual mother to all who will listen.

The messages from the Blessed Virgin found throughout the book are given exactly as presented to the visionaries. They are found at the end of each chapter as well as within them. One full chapter is devoted to the most revealing, shocking and inspiring messages given in the early days of her appearances in the village. These early encounters were singularly vital in acceptance of her messages, first by the villagers and then by the world. If belief and acceptance had

---

3 One of the 10 Commandments: You shall not kill. That means literally we are not to take the God-given gift of life in any way.

not initially occurred with the villagers, the apparitions would have in all likelihood faded away.

Where better to begin the journey of discovery about the last apparitions of the Mother of Jesus then by clarifying why she is the messenger sent to deliver these implausible messages to the world. And why not—she is a mother.

*Dear children! Give thanks with me to the Most High for my presence with you. My heart is joyful watching the love and joy in the living of my messages. Many of you have responded, but I wait for, and seek, all the hearts that have fallen asleep to awaken from the sleep of unbelief. Little children, draw even closer to my Immaculate Heart so that I can lead all of you toward eternity. Thank you for having responded to my call.*

—Message given to Medjugorje visionary Marija on June 25, 2011.

> And a great portent appeared in heaven: a woman clothed with the sun, with the moon under her feet, and on her head a crown of twelve stars. She was pregnant and was crying out in birth pangs, in the agony of giving birth.
>
> —Revelation 12:1-2.

## CHAPTER II: HEAVEN'S MESSENGER

WHY IS the Blessed Virgin Mary the one sent to deliver the last apparitional messages from Heaven that will change the world forever? Why not Jesus Himself; or, one of the biblical prophets, such as Moses or Elijah?

The answer to the question usually put forth by non-Catholics can be found in Holy Scripture, the sure way to discern the truth of any claimed supernatural grace allegedly coming from Heaven. I am indebted to Doctor Mark Miravalle, a noted Marian theologian and co-author of our book *Are the Medjugorje Apparitions Authentic?*. It is his profound, yet simple explanations, which clearly describe why the Blessed Virgin plays so powerful a role in spiritual conversion of the world. Many of his theological conclusions about Mary's role are used in this chapter.

Most Christian theologians today acknowledge that the "woman clothed with the sun" referred to in Holy Scripture is the chosen mother of Jesus Christ. This single piece of scripture offers a fundamental reason to accept the premise that the Blessed Virgin Mary received a *second* major role in God's plan of salvation for His creation: To be the *spiritual* mother of the children of God. This second role singularly gives reason enough to accept her as the harbinger of such an ultra-critical message through her appearance at the little village.

Confirmation of Mary's second role comes from the same book and chapter in Revelation. Verse 17 states: **Then the dragon was angry with the woman, and went off to make war on the rest of her children, those who keep the commandments of God and hold the testimony of Jesus.** The narrative of the Book of Revelation, credited to have been written by the disciple John, goes on to make clear that his reference is to Mary by writing in the fifth verse: **And she gave birth to a son, a male child, who is to rule all the nations with a rod of iron.** That Son, of course, is Jesus.

The reference to "her children" are the children of God—all of the children of God, including those who have not yet accepted His gift of salvation, and who do not as yet keep the commandments of God. A natural progression is to see Mary as the messenger sent throughout the centuries in supernatural apparition to assure that all of her spiritual children will at least have an opportunity through the grace of free will to respond to and accept the teachings of Jesus. The summation of her 31-plus years of teaching messages at Medjugorje is to prepare us for what has been prophesized for centuries—the will of God on earth as it is in Heaven. That is why Medjugorje will be the last apparition site of the Blessed Virgin Mary on earth.

Mary's first role undoubtedly is to be the chosen Mother of our God who comes to earth as a helpless human baby. However, Jesus confirms her second role at the height of His indescribable suffering. He looks down from the cross at His mother standing with his beloved disciple John. We can only imagine the agony of actually speaking through such suffering as He utters, **"Woman, here is your son!"** and to John, **"Here is your mother!"**[1]

The theological question is this: Would a suffering Jesus take this particular time to address a domestic chore by asking His disciple John to physically care for His mother from that time on? Would He not have taken care of such a task before His death? It makes far more sense to see this drama as Jesus *assigning* His human mother Mary as the spiritual mother to all humanity, with His disciple John standing in for all of us. It is confirmed by the obvious; *every word uttered by Jesus from the cross was done with explicit, meaningful purpose.*

Many Protestants visiting Medjugorje, as well as those of other beliefs, have risen above traditional teachings of individual faiths concerning Mary to acknowledge this second role. They have accepted the "Blessed Mother" as an integral part of their pathway to her Son. That includes the author of this book who at the time of discovering Medjugorje was at best a lukewarm Lutheran Protestant.

We can also reference the Old Testament as significant proof of the role of Mary as spiritual mother. In Genesis, chapter three, verse 15: **I will put enmity between you and the woman, and between your offspring and hers; he will strike your head, and you will strike his heel.'** Again, the "woman" is attributed to be the Blessed Virgin Mary. It cannot be a reference to Eve; she has already sinned, so it is not possible for her to have enmity, that is, total and unmitigated opposition toward evil. The offspring is Jesus who will do battle with Satan for the souls of his creation.

---

1 John 19;25-27; New Testament.

Is Mary just "another fish" selected from the sea of humanity to become the mother of the Living God? Hardly. We turn to Holy Scripture again to see just who this woman really is. There are two prophecies in the Old Testament that foretell the *Virgin* birth of Jesus. This is an important point as to who she is and why she is titled the Blessed Virgin Mary. The first is in Isaiah 7:14: **Therefore the Lord himself will give you a sign. Look, the young woman is with child and shall bear a son, and shall name him Immanuel.** Later in the chapter, Immanuel (which means, "God is with us") is referred to as the future savior of his people, which connects the prophecy even more clearly to the Virgin Mary and Jesus. Then, in the Book of Micah 5:2-3,[2] the prophet foretells the birth of the savior in Bethlehem from a "woman who will bring forth the ruler of Israel".

Throughout the New Testament, the focus is overwhelmingly on Jesus as it should be. It is not on His human mother, with the exception of a handful of verses and references. The reason for this is obvious: Jesus is God. Mary is His human mother; she is not a goddess. She can perform no miracles. If the divine nature of Jesus was not clearly and solidly established in Holy Scripture, devotion to the Blessed Virgin Mary simply would not make sense. She is, in essence, His human mother and as so, is to be *venerated*[3] purely because of that role.

---

2  But you, O Bethlehem of Ephrata, who are one of the little clans of Judah, from you shall come forth for me one who is to rule in Israel, whose origin is from of old, from ancient days.
3  Therefore he shall give them up until the time when she who is in labor has brought forth; then the rest of his kindred shall return to the people of Israel.
3  To venerate is to regard one with feelings of respect and reverence. A good example is how we regard our family members. We do not worship them even though we use that expression as a term of love.

The limited reference to the Blessed Virgin Mary in scripture adds to the mystique surrounding her. It adds to her profound humility, a necessary trait to fulfill the dual role of mother to God and to humanity. One final reference gives consolidation to all quoted Holy Scripture about Mary. It is from the New Testament Book of Luke, chapter one, beginning with verse 26: **In the sixth month the angel Gabriel was sent by God to a town in Galilee called Nazareth, to a virgin engaged to a man whose name was Joseph, of the house of David. The virgin's name was Mary. And he came to her and said, 'Greetings, favored one! The Lord is with you.'**

Later in the chapter, Mary sets out and goes to the home of Zechariah and Elizabeth, the parents of John, The Baptist, who will be the precursor of the Messiah. As she enters the tiny courtyard, Elizabeth who is filled with the Holy Spirit exclaims with a cry, **"And why has this happened to me, that the mother of my Lord comes to me?**

Mary's response to Elizabeth brings the entirety of her role as mother to God and to His creation. Her answer, known as the "Magnificat" is as follows:

**And Mary said, "My soul magnifies the Lord, and my spirit rejoices in God my Savior, for He has looked with favor on the lowliness of his servant. Surely, from now on all generations will call me blessed; for the Mighty One has done great things for me, and holy is his name. His mercy is for those who fear him from generation to generation. He has shown strength with his arm; he has scattered the proud in the thoughts of their hearts. He has brought down the powerful from their thrones, and lifted up the lowly; he has filled the hungry with good things, and sent the rich away empty. He has helped his servant Israel, in remembrance of**

**his mercy, according to the promise he made to our ancestors, to Abraham and to his descendants for ever.'**

Therefore, Mary, the messenger of Medjugorje is according to Holy Scripture the *daughter* of the Father, the *bride* of the Holy Spirit and the *mother* of the Son of God. Thus, it is reasonable to accept her as a messenger from Heaven—the Messenger of Medjugorje. There is little doubt of the crisis that prompts Heaven to send her to earth at this time. There is also ample evidence to see her as a prophet of these times.

Let us see how the hope for the world will change it forever, when Mary, the spiritual mother, once again is sent to earth in apparition.

*Dear children! Today I call you to pray and fast for my intentions, because Satan wants to destroy my plan. Here I began with this parish and invited the entire world. Many have responded, but there is an enormous number of those who do not want to hear or accept my call. Therefore, you who have said 'yes', be strong and resolute. Thank you for having responded to my call.*

—Message given to visionary Marija in Medjugorje on August 25, 2011.

> And Mary said, "Behold, I am the handmaid of the Lord; let it be done
> to me according to your word. "And the angel departed from her.
>
> —Luke, Chapter 1:38.

## CHAPTER III: HOPE FOR THE WORLD

NESTLED IN the rugged mountains of Bosnia-Hercegovina, the village of Medjugorje is now world famous stemming from the on-going supernatural apparitions of the Blessed Virgin Mary. It began on June 24, 1981 and continues to occur daily to three of the six seers as of this writing. The content and nature of the messages the Virgin gives arguably qualifies this as one of the most urgent and important events occurring today. Millions of followers believe it is the last hope for the world.

The messages are highlighted by 10 prophecies or "secrets" as they are generally called (how I will refer to them). These mysterious secrets concern future cataclysmic events that will change the world. The Virgin stated in the early days of the apparitions that she would randomly reveal the secrets to the young seers as she continued to appear to them over time. Once a visionary receives all 10 secrets, the Virgin no longer appears to them daily, but promises to appear to them at least once a year or in times of extreme agony caused by the knowledge of the secrets and what they contain. According to the visionaries, many of the secrets are catastrophic in nature.

Adding to the urgency, three of the six visionaries have received all 10 secrets and no longer have the daily apparition. The remaining three seers have received nine secrets each. When each one of the remaining three will receive the tenth and last secret is known only by Heaven.

An added, unprecedented occurrence began in 1987, when one of the visionaries, Mirjana Ivankovic, who had received all of the secrets and stopped having the daily apparition, started receiving apparitions again on the second day of each month. The new apparitions were to be kept private at the request of the Virgin until February 2, 1997. They are primarily directed at those who do not believe in God, but also as a reminder for all. They are blunt and to the point; yet, they are gentle and filled with concern. When the last remaining active visionary (or visionaries) receives the tenth and final secret, there will be a brief period before the first one occurs, followed by the others with short time intervals between them.

The Virgin has made clear that when the first three secrets take place, which are actually warnings to the world, *all living souls from that moment on* will know the full truth of the reality of God. No one will be able to deny His existence. There will no longer be reason for division of beliefs in an omnipotent Creator of the universe. Humanity will be one global family under the guidance of the living Son of God, Jesus Christ.

Even with the incomprehensible grace given to all living humans, there will be those who will continue to ignore or reject God. It will be too late for them to convert after the third secret/warning is revealed to the world.

The primary objective of the apparitions according to the Blessed Virgin is not to frighten or threaten people, but to bring them back to God. She revealed early in her appearances that these would be her *final* apparitions on earth because, as she said in an early message to the visionaries, *it will no longer be necessary.* This revelation by the prophet of our time is the second key reason to consider the apparitions at Medjugorje to be the most important event occurring in the world.

In the more than 2000-year history of the Roman Catholic Church, the Blessed Virgin Mary has appeared in apparition numerous times. The most notable sites of past apparitions include Guadalupe, Mexico (1531); Rue du Bac, in Paris, France (1830); La Salette, France (1846) and Lourdes, France (1858); and, Fatima, Portugal (1917). Today, there are many other claimed apparitions happening throughout the world. Some of them are compatible with what is given at Medjugorje, while many are questionable.

It is vitally important to explore some past apparitions to see how they relate to Medjugorje. The apparitions at Fatima are the clearest example; it is notably the most critical of apparition sites before Medjugorje. The Virgin stated in her early Medjugorje messages that what she is giving there is a continuation and fulfillment of what she gave to the children at Fatima.

The evidence of the singular importance of Medjugorje lies in the fact that never in the history of Marian apparitions has the Blessed Virgin Mary appeared daily for so long a period of time, to so many visionaries with such profound global impact. She has made her purpose clear by stating in the first days of her appearance: The world must turn to God for the only true peace and happiness.

The messages given at Medjugorje represent a culmination of all that has come before in the Virgin's apparitions. When they began in the summer of 1981, the civil struggles of the Federation of

Yugoslavia represented a microcosm of the modern world plagued by social injustice and the threat of war. For centuries, the region had been ripped apart by the mutual antagonisms of its three distinct ethnic groups: Croatians (the predominant group living in and around Medjugorje), Serbians and Muslims. Their history had been one of nearly constant clashes between the three. Every succeeding generation suffered from an endless cycle of invasion, resistance, and brief liberation.

Between periods of conquest by outsiders, the three groups practiced war on each other. An anguished history of hate-filled, reciprocating atrocities among them was only quelled following World War II through the forced unity of an atheistic, Marxist dictatorship run with brute authority by Josip Tito. Six Slavic republics, including Croatia and Serbia, became the forced Federation of Yugoslavia. Ironically, Tito who was Croatian was raised a Catholic.

Despite the sensation of the Blessed Virgin's apparitions in the region, the people as a whole did not initially heed her urgent call to reconciliation. It was not due to belief or unbelief in the apparitions but the fact that Catholic Croat and Orthodox Serb could not and did not want to live with each other. Neither could stand the converted Muslim Slav, created out of four centuries of Turkish rule. Eventually, with the swift fall of Communism in the early nineties, it led to a bloody and horrible civil war beginning in the spring of 1991. It raged on into the better part of 1995. Hundreds of thousands of refugees from all ethnic groups were the innocent victims. Damage to cities, towns and villages will take decades to restore. It was one of, if not the most *evil* war of the 20th century.

Yet, throughout this horrific struggle, the Virgin continued to appear in Medjugorje. Amazingly, no damage was done to the village during the war while destruction and death came to all areas surrounding it. The sad irony is that the Blessed Virgin came to Medjugorje calling herself the Queen of Peace with the stated intent early on to lead the people to peaceful co-existence. Few listened.

The presence of the Madonna through the apparitions did indeed bring many to conversion. Pilgrims came to Medjugorje from all over the world even during the height of the conflict. They came not just for personal spiritual reasons but also to bring desperately needed material aid to hapless victims of the war. Many who came were those who had previously been to Medjugorje on pilgrimage; now they returned without regard to personal danger or possible death. This response by people to the Medjugorje messages serves as powerful evidence of the effects of its spiritual message. It is a vivid reflection of the biblical parable where the good seed falls into fertile soil and gives off a hundred-fold.

It is important to note that the Blessed Virgin appears to Catholic youths in Medjugorje, all of whom are now married and parents. As in the beginning days, her messages today still generally ask adherence to the sacraments of the Roman Catholic Church. That is not by accident since only Roman Catholics and those of the orthodox faiths venerate and acknowledge her as the Mother of God. However, she has made clear from the beginning that her messages were for people of *all* beliefs. The *sincerity* of belief and *adherence* to the moral law of God by followers of all human-created religions is her overriding request.

A critical element that stresses the point that the Blessed Virgin Mary is sent from heaven for everyone came when she gave one of the most vital messages in January 1985. It came about when a Croatian Catholic priest doubted the healing of a Serbian gypsy child. How, he asked one of the visionaries in obvious nationalistic dismay, could the Mother of God intercede for the healing of a child of the Orthodox faith of the despised ethnic enemy, the Serbians?

The question was put to the Virgin by one of the visionaries. The seer reported that the Virgin looked at the priest for a long time before answering. It was not a gaze of repulsion, as one might imagine in human terms; rather, it was that of a long-suffering mother with endless tolerance. This was her response: *Tell this priest; tell everyone, that it is you who are divided on earth. The Muslims and the Orthodox, for the same reason as Catholics, are equal before my Son and me. You are all my children. Certainly, all religions are not equal, but all men are equal before God, as St. Paul says. It does not suffice to belong to the Catholic Church to be saved, but it is necessary to respect the commandments of God in following one's conscience.*

As if the clarity and common sense wisdom in the beginning part of this critical message from the Blessed Virgin was not enough, she continued with even more astounding truths: *Those who are not Catholics are no less creatures made in the image of God, and destined to rejoin someday the House of the Father. Salvation is available to everyone, without exception. Only those who refuse God deliberately are condemned. To him who has been given little, little will be asked for. To whomever has been given much, very much will be required. It is God alone, in His infinite justice, who determines the degree of responsibility* (for each person) *and pronounces judgment.*

It would take an extended period of study and meditation, as well as endless discussion among a group of theologians from all faiths to comprehend all that the Blessed Mother is saying in this message. Yet, it is solidly grounded in Scripture. The simple, yet profound point is obvious: We are all the children of God.

The beginning of the last apparition by the Madonna began on a warm day in June 1981. Life in the little rural village of Medjugorje was about to change forever. Its change would eventually bring about changes throughout the world.

*Dear children! Today I am calling you to a complete surrender to God. Everything you do and everything you possess give over to God so that He can take control in your life as the King of all that you possess. That way, through me, God can lead you into the depths of the spiritual life. Little children, do not be afraid, because I am with you even if you think there is no way out and that Satan is in control. I am bringing peace to you. I am your mother, the Queen of Peace. I am blessing you with the blessings of joy so that for you God may be everything in your life. Thank you for having responded to my call.*

—Message given to visionary Marija on July 25, 1983.

> To him the gatekeeper opens; the sheep hear his voice, and he calls his own sheep by name and leads them out. When he has brought out all his own, he goes before them, and the sheep follow him, for they know his voice.
>
> —John 10:3-4.

## CHAPTER IV: ON A WARM DAY IN JUNE

UNDERSTANDING HOW the apparitions at Medjugorje began is critical in accepting it as something that is of the greatest importance for the entire world. Without comprehension of its formation, acceptance and subsequent impact, there is little basis to believe it.

I have written the story of how the apparitions began in my earlier books, as have many others. Much of the original story is necessarily contained here. The importance of its retelling is centered on showing how many contrasting elements would play important roles in bringing about success to Heaven's final call to conversion. It is also necessary to tell how it began for those who know nothing about Medjugorje or past apparitions of the Mother of God. The reader familiar with my writings and telling of the story will also find far greater depth of critical details and new information that further clarify its overall mission.

The reaction of the local and regional Communist government authorities was the catalyst that fueled the primary force determined to destroy the apparitions before it advanced into a legitimate threat to its power. Would they be successful in crushing something they viewed as a full insurrection against the Communist government? Even more critical would be the response of the local bishop and his successor. Above all, the reaction and immediate acceptance by the villagers would be the crux of success in allowing mankind one more chance to accept the grace of salvation from God through the intercession of the Blessed Virgin Mary.

### Praise be to Jesus Christ!

The figure of a beautiful young woman in a shimmering brilliance of light with arms upraised smiled as she softly uttered these words to the six youths kneeling before her. It was June 25, 1981, the *second* day she had appeared in apparition in the village. Every incredible visit they would have with her from that day on would begin with these same words.

The greeting from the Virgin Mary is more than a greeting. It serves as immediate evidence that the entity the youth were seeing was indeed the Mother of Jesus and not a demonic spirit. The proof lies in the fact that Satan and his demons cannot utter such words of praise for Jesus. This was later borne out by Satan's attempt to deceive one of the new visionaries, Mirjana Dragecevic, by appearing to her on two separate occasions looking exactly as the Blessed Virgin Mary looked when she appeared to her. Only when he did not offer the greeting did Mirjana know it was not the Madonna.

There was quite a crowd of local villagers witnessing the sight of the six young Croatians kneeling in front of what they described as a beautiful young woman. It marked the first of what would develop into thousands of supernatural conversations between her and the six Croatian children chosen to be visionaries. Word had spread that she might appear again and nearly 100 villagers had come to see what would happen. Most of them had come out of curiosity having heard about the children's claim the day before. Of course, only the young seers could see her. The villagers knelt in prayer around them, asking for personal intentions and hoping by some miracle that all of this was real.

The initial apparition of the Blessed Virgin had actually occurred the day before on June 24. It was a special day for the faithful of the local Catholic Church, the feast day of Saint John, The Baptist. Mary's first apparition in Medjugorje on a feast day of the Church is no coincidence. She would verify through her messages over the ensuing years that everything in the way of spiritual conversion is done according to Heaven's plan. There are no coincidences.

The Virgin's opening appearance on the feast day of John the Baptist, the greatest prophet ever according to the words of Jesus in Holy Scripture, was indeed intentional. Like John, Mary was Heaven's special messenger calling for repentance and a return to God in these modern times.

A surprised sixteen-year-old Ivanka Ivankovic was the first to see the vision. She described the experience as suddenly seeing three flashes of a brilliant light on the side of a hill above where she and her close friend Mirjana, 15, were walking. It was unlike any light she had seen before. In the midst of its brilliance was the image of a beautiful young woman holding an infant in her arms. Ivanka immediately knew in her heart that it was the Blessed Virgin Mary. Despite the crushing oppression of the local Communist government, faith amongst the people remained strong.

Mirjana did not see the flashes of light or the image of the woman. She had drifted ahead of her friend lost in her own thoughts as they made their way toward their homes. Upon seeing the vision,

Ivanka excitedly shouted to her friend that "Gospa" [1] was appearing on the side of the hill. Mirjana did not believe her and refused to look, thinking that her friend was simply playing a trick on her as they often did to each other. She was mildly upset that Ivanka would joke about something holy. With a wry smile, she answered her friend without turning around. "Sure, Our Lady has nothing better to do. Besides, why would she appear to us? We're no better than anyone else!"

After a few moments, a very serious Ivanka ran after Mirjana and convinced her she was not joking. She begged her to return to the spot where she saw the figure. Mirjana quickly returned with her. She was astounded to be able to see the image as well. They were soon joined by several other young people who also were able to see the beautiful young woman in the light. Some of them could see her clearly while others only saw a cloudy or hazy figure.

The vision of the young woman hovering about fifty yards up the side of the small hill smiled continuously as she beckoned to them to come to her. They were too frightened to respond. The figure would motion to them to come to her while covering and uncovering an infant in her arms, whom she would later reveal to be the child Jesus. Several of the youth fell to their knees and started praying; others began to weep. Soon-to-be visionary Ivan Dragicevic (no relation to Mirjana), 17, who had come upon the scene with a companion minutes after it began, took a quick look and ran away. Another girl, Vicka Ivankovic, 17, who was a close friend of Ivanka and Mirjana, and who would also become one of the visionaries, had

---

1 The affectionate Croatian term for "Our Lady".

come to the site just after Ivan; she, too, ran away, thinking the others were seeing a snake.

As the rain intensified, the youth slowly backed away from the scene, then turned and swiftly ran to their homes where they excitedly told family and friends what had happened. It did not take long for the news to spread through the small community: Gospa had appeared in their village.

Hardly anyone, including family members, actually believed the young people who would soon be world-famous as visionaries. They were chided by family members not to joke about the Virgin Mary appearing to them, and teased by friends that maybe they had seen a flying saucer or a ghost. Others went so far as to suggest that possibly they were experimenting with drugs. Despite the teasing and rebukes, the new seers steadfastly stuck to their story.

The following day, June 25, some of the youths who had seen the vision the previous day felt an irresistible inner urge to return to the scene. Leading the group were Mirjana and Ivanka. They persuaded their good friend Vicka to come with them. One young girl, 13-year-old Milka Pavlovic who had briefly seen the Virgin on the first day was too far away working in the field with her mother. She, too, felt the inner urge.

When Ivanka and Mirjana went looking for Milka at her home and found that she was not there, her sister Marija, 16, and a cousin, little nine-year-old Jakov Colo, pleaded with the two girls to come and get them if the Gospa appeared again. When the figure did appear again, Vicka ran the short distance to Marija's home to bring them to the site.

Thus, on the second day of the apparitions the six Croatian teens who would become the Medjugorje visionaries were together for the first time. There was Ivanka, the first to see the Virgin, followed by Mirjana. They were joined by Vicka, who had run home that first day. In place of Milka was her sister Marija who had come with little Jakov. Lastly, there was Ivan who had run home after briefly seeing her the first day and locked himself in his room, frightened that the Virgin might appear to him again at any moment.

As the six youths looked at the spot on the hill, the figure appeared again after the three flashes of light. This time she did not have the infant in her arms. When she beckoned to them to come to her, the young people raced up the side of the bramble-covered, rocky slopes at a speed beyond their physical ability. A climb that normally would take twelve to fifteen minutes was accomplished in only two. They knelt less than five feet away from the image as the Virgin greeted them with those special words: *Praise be to Jesus Christ!*

The children stared in awe. They were actually seeing the Blessed Virgin Mary and she was literally speaking to them. In the initial moment of being in front of the Virgin, Marija and little Jakov could see her as the others saw her but not as clearly; but they could not hear her speaking. That would change the following day when all six of the selected visionaries could see and hear her exactly the same.

The visionaries would later describe that they saw the Blessed Virgin Mary in a three-dimensional way, just as we see each other, they would explain. She was described as looking very Croatian, about nineteen to twenty-one years of age, approximately 5' 7" tall, slender in form, and indescribably beautiful beyond any statue or picture they had ever seen. She had blue eyes, a pale alabaster white complexion, with a small curl of black hair showing on the left side of her face from under a long white veil that reached down in length to a small white cloud that covered her feet. The cloud, the children stated, grew with the length of time the Virgin remained in apparition. Her dress was described as long, without a sash, and of a lucent, silver-gray color. In addition, they added, she had a crown of twelve stars circling her head.[2]

Mirjana then asked The Virgin a telling question: "Why are you appearing to us? We are no better than others." The Virgin smiled and paused before answering: *I do not necessarily choose the best* (people).

The visionaries, villagers and visiting pilgrims would only understand this response later. God chooses ordinary people for extraordinary missions. Those chosen for a supernatural grace, which allows them to see a heavenly visitor, are chosen not because of the good they may have done in the past or present but for the good they can do in the future.

The first conversational apparition of the Blessed Virgin Mary lasted for what seemed to the young visionaries a long time; they did not want it to end. One of them finally asked her, "Will you come back?" *Yes*, the Virgin responded, *to the same place as yesterday.*

Mirjana quickly added, "Dear Gospa, they will not believe us when we go home. They will tell us that we are crazy. Please give a sign (that you are really appearing to us)." The Virgin simply smiled and then said, *Goodbye my angels. Go in God's peace.*

By the third day, Friday, June 26, it seemed as if the entire region knew about the apparitions at Medjugorje. A crowd of more than three thousand people filling every part of the hill reacted as

---

2 John 19:25-27, NRSV Bible. The Blessed Virgin Mary is described as having a crown of twelve stars in Revelation 12:1: "And a great portent appeared in heaven, a woman clothed with the sun, with the moon under her feet, and on her head a crown of twelve stars . . ."

the visionaries knelt again in a state of ecstasy. The crowd pressed in on the young people causing concern for their safety. People shouted questions to the visionaries to ask of the Virgin, most for specific cures of conditions and diseases for family members. Emotion-driven confusion soon reigned.

Even though all of the seers were sure by this time that this was the Blessed Virgin Mary, they were thrilled when Vicka doused her with holy water and said, "If you are from God, stay; but, if you are from Satan, be gone!" the Virgin smiled and remained with them. Emboldened, they began to ask questions that many people had requested including the priests: Who are you? Why have you come? What do you want?

The Blessed Virgin Mary began answering: *My dear children, I am the Blessed Virgin Mary* and *I have come to tell you that God exists and that He loves you. I have come because there are many true believers here. I wish to be with you to convert and to reconcile the whole world.*

When the apparition was over the crowd pressed in on the visionaries and they became separated from each other. Marija started making her way down the mobbed pathway accompanied by a young man who was a neighbor. What happened next gave primary purpose to the Virgin's reason for appearing at this specific site in the region.

Finally separated from the mob of people and quickly making her way down the hill, Marija suddenly felt a mysterious tug that moved her to the left side of the trail where once again the Virgin appeared to her. The radiant happiness of the beautiful young woman surrounded by light just minutes earlier was now replaced by somber concern. She hovered in front of the image of an empty grey cross, hands folded together and tears pouring down her cheeks as she pleaded to the young visionary: *Peace! Peace! Peace! Be reconciled! Only Peace! Make your peace with God and among yourselves. For that, it is necessary to believe, to pray, to fast, and to go to confession.*

The powerful second message given to Marija on the first day of intimate conversation with the Mother of God was a pointed warning not only for the three ethnic groups that formed the population of Yugoslavia, but most emphatically for the entire world. It was in essence the core reason for her appearing there at this particular time. If the messages were accepted and peace was to come to the area, then it would also apply for the entire world. Without a positive response, the mission of Medjugorje would fail.

The first days of the apparitions would prove to be crucial to its overall success in converting the world back to the ways of God. Of course, it was not noticeable at the time. It would have to begin with acceptance by the villagers and response in a positive light to set the stage for what could be the greatest Marian apparition in the history of the Church.

With the long tradition of animosity between Croats, Serbs and Muslims, it would be a miracle if peace were to reign. As the apparitions continued each day, there was no guarantee it would happen.

*Dear children! Today again I am calling you to prayer and fasting. You know, dear children, that with your help I am able to accomplish everything and force Satan not to be seducing to evil and to remove himself from this place. Dear children, Satan is lurking for each in-*

*dividual. Especially in everyday affairs he wants to spread confusion among each one of you. Therefore, dear children, my call to you is that your day would be only prayer and complete surrender to God. Thank you for having responded to my call."*

—General message to the visionaries given on September 4, 1986.

You are the light of the world. A city built on a hill cannot be hidden. No one after lighting a lamp puts it under the bushel basket, but on the lampstand, and it gives light to all in the house. In the same way, let your light shine before others, so that they may see your good works and give glory to your Father in heaven.

—Matthew 5:14-16.

## CHAPTER V: CRITICAL FIRST DAYS

THE FIRST DAYS of the Blessed Virgin's visits, days that would determine its success or failure, brought about dramatic actions. Only later would these formative days be seen as crucial to the overall success of the apparitions. Would the villagers become "the light of the world"? It was during this time that the key elements and individual roles necessary to its survival and eventual impact were defined. For the success of the apparitions, the people had to become the example that would "let their light shine before others".

It would not come easy.

For the quiet hamlet of Bijakovici, one of the five small hamlets that made up the village of Medjugorje and the geographical point where it was all happening, the sudden occurrence of the daily apparitions was traumatizing to the normal routine of daily life. It was happening too swiftly to comprehend what it meant and how it would affect the community in the future.

Thousands of people were suddenly coming to once-obscure Medjugorje. The crowds grew by quantum leaps. Each day they surged through the narrow streets of the tiny hamlet on their way to the hill for the evening apparition. The pattern of life that had been nearly the same for centuries changed—abruptly and permanently.

Pandemonium accompanied each day of the continuing apparitions. The first important step was to establish a workable routine out of the necessity to protect the young seers and give a semblance of order to the new way of life. Every evening at approximately 6:30, the visionaries would gather at a spot high on the local hill usually used for the daily tending of the villagers' sheep. It was just above the original site where the Virgin had first appeared in an area rarely visited because it was so high with rocky, bramble-covered slopes. Now every crevice in the rugged terrain was filled with people who surrounded the visionaries as close as possible. They were held at bay by a hastily appointed group of men whose duty was to protect them.

Numerous cries from the visionaries warned the crowds that they were actually stepping on the edge of the gown of the Blessed Virgin. "Be careful!" they would shout to those too close to the spot where she was standing. "You are standing on parts of her gown and she keeps disappearing each time you do that!"

Following a period of prayer led by the visionaries, the Blessed Virgin would appear after three sudden bursts of brilliant light that was sometimes visible to some in the crowd. The visionaries would then fall to their knees in synchronization. Their group prayer would stop on exactly the same word and their eyes would focus on the spot where the Virgin was evidently appearing. Each visionary would seem to be in conversation with her, separate from the others. Their mouths moved to form words but without audible sound to the onlookers.

The apparition would last for various times ranging from a few minutes to an hour. It depended, the visionaries explained, on the needs presented and the teachings of the Virgin during the time of the apparition. The children were in a light state of ecstasy neither hearing or seeing anyone but the Blessed Virgin. Afterwards they would return to normal and then describe the experience to the people and answer their questions as best they could. On some occasions, they would come in and out of the ecstasy several times during the apparition.

Everyone wanted the teenage visionaries to plead their individual needs before the Virgin. Many were surprisingly successful. Miracles occurred from the smallest of requested things to healings of major infirmities. There were incredible healings of physical and psychological conditions. The good fruits of the apparitions fueled credence that it was authentic and truly a gift of grace from God.

Proof of the first magnitude that the apparitions were a unique grace from Heaven was galvanized by one of the most implausible revelations given through the newly chosen visionary, 16-year-old Ivanka Ivankovic. It transpired on the first day of conversation with the Virgin (June 25). She had lost her mother just a little more than a month before the apparitions began. Ivanka's mother had been rushed to the hospital in the nearby city of Mostar with a serious illness but no one had expected her death. Her daughter was left lonely and depressed. Now the young girl was on the hill overlooking her home, able to see and converse with a beautiful lady who claimed to be from Heaven.

Ivanka's question was inevitable: "Dear Lady, where is my mother?"

The Virgin's answer filled the young seer with unbounded joy: *Your mother is in heaven with us!*

It was astounding news that reverberated through the village and surrounding communities. Belief that these apparitions were indeed from God spread at a rapid rate. From this initial revelation given on the first of these ten critical beginning days, came a revealing question: How could this woman go straight to heaven when she had done nothing particularly special in life?

The answer was simple. Ivanka's mother had been a good wife and mother. She had lived her faith daily with prayers and frequent attendance at Mass, accepting what God had given her in life and fulfilling the responsibility that came with it. The Blessed Virgin would emphasize these basic requirements for holiness through her ensuing messages.

Two days later, Ivanka, still thrilled with the response to her question on the first day concerning her mother, dared to ask another: "Dear Lady, do you have a message for me from my mother?" The Virgin smiled and responded: *Behave well and obey your grandmother. Help her because she is elderly.* Ivanka smiled and vigorously nodded her head in the affirmative.

The story of Ivanka's mother immediately created near-uncontrollable crowds on the little hill. Out of this chaotic beginning came the most important development during the decisive ten days of its beginning. The local church leaders became concerned with the overwhelming crowds invading their little parish. They were reluctantly forced to become involved. The people needed solid, spiritual leadership—and a thorough investigation of the apparitions in order to initiate a proper course of reaction. Making matters worse, the local pastor was away at a retreat and not due back for several days.

The initial response among the associate Franciscan priests stationed at Saint James Church to the youths' claims of seeing the Madonna daily ranged from total rejection, to timid acceptance that it could be true. None of them seemed to know quite what to do about it. One priest suggested exorcism but that step was immediately rejected. After long sessions of questioning the youths, another priest finally urged them to request a sign from the Virgin to prove that the apparitions were really from God. The Virgin's answer was calm and direct: *Blessed are those who have not seen and who believe.*

How could the priests counter such a response, which fell directly in line with Holy Scripture? Yet, many remained unconvinced. The teenagers continued to be questioned sharply in long sessions by the Franciscans, who desperately hoped their pastor might have a plan to deal with this apparition business when he returned.

Father Jozo Zovko had been the pastor at Medjugorje for only ten months. He was an intense, holy, traditional priest, strict in his duties and known for long homilies laced with theology above the full understanding of most of the parishioners. He was far too handsome to be a priest in the eyes of many of the women in the parish. The always-serious pastor returned to the parish at noon on Saturday, June 27, to discover the uproar.

Father Jozo remained cautious after immediately learning most of what had happened up to that point from his assistant pastor and the Franciscan nuns stationed in the parish. Who were the children who made these claims, he asked. When he discovered that one of them, Mirjana, was from the city of Sarajevo and only visiting in Medjugorje for the summer, he became suspicious. The fact that he did not even know the other local teens involved only added to his skepticism. Maybe this whole nonsense about apparitions was indeed a trick thought up by the Communists and forced onto the six youths to find further reason to harass the Church. Possibly the outsider, Mirjana, had brought drugs to the village and induced the others to try  them with her. At this stage, all such thoughts had some relevancy.

At approximately the same time the information about the event was being given to Father Jozo, the visionaries were forcibly being taken by the local police to the small town of Citluk, three miles from their village. It was the headquarters for the Communist government authorities who demanded the children be examined medically to determine whether they had been under the influence of drugs. Their purpose once again was fueled by suspicions of a possible uprising against the atheistic government locally and regionally.

The medical staff cleared the youths from any influence of drugs, but the authorities decided to take them to the city of Mostar for further examinations. When informed of this, the children refused and quickly left the health clinic where they were being held.  Fortunately, they immediately ran into a villager from Medjugorje who owned a minivan and had come to the area for some shopping; seeing the children so upset, he quickly returned them to the village.

The children had the villager drop them off directly at the church hoping that Father Jozo had returned. They desperately wanted to sit with him and explain all that had happened from their perspective. The pastor immediately met with them and the seers were filled with joy. At last, they could share their experiences with their priest. He would believe them.

To their dismay, Father Jozo remained aloof and insisted on speaking to each of them privately.  By this method, he could compare what each had to say. He could then check one against the other to be sure they were telling the truth. The priest was taking all means necessary to remain objective and protect the integrity of the Church.

After an exhaustive session with Father Jozo, the visionaries returned to their homes to rest for a brief period before going to the hill for the daily apparition. That evening, they asked the Blessed Virgin what she wanted from the priests. Her reply: *Let the priests strongly believe and protect the faith of their people.* They then asked why she would not just appear to all of the people so that no one could question their integrity. The Virgin repeated what she had said when the priests had asked the visionaries to ask for a sign to prove she was appearing to them: *Blessed are those who believe and yet do not see.* She then added, *Let them believe in the same way as they would if they were able to see me.*

The interviews with the children only caused further confusion for Father Jozo. He was at least partially convinced that they were possibly sincere and actually believed what was happening to them. How could a little 10-year-old boy, Jakov, make up such stories and stick to them in the face of stern interrogation? Their individual stories varied in small detail but that only added to his growing belief that they were telling the truth. Still, if this was from God, why were the people not coming to the church and praying? Why were they running to the hill instead? After much thought and prayer, he decided to issue a statement to the parish.

Day five of the apparitions was a Sunday with two scheduled Masses. Father Jozo gathered the other parish priests to come up with the proper wording for the statement to be read at the Masses. The statement assured the faithful that the situation was being closely monitored. It cautioned the parishioners not to be driven by curiosity. The seers were being protected and further investigation was being conducted. The most important thing was to pray and allow the Church time to come up with some answers.

Father Jozo also used his homily in an attempt to quell the curiosity of the villagers and to lead them to focus on the spirituality. "Yes, it is true that God can appear to men and God had been appearing in the past," he said. "It is also true that Our Lady can appear and she has appeared in the past as well, but we do not need these signs, for we have Jesus right here, in the Holy Eucharist!"

It was vintage Father Jozo: focus on the spiritual, the reality of the presence of Jesus in the Church—not on the curious or sensational things of which you cannot be sure.

After the morning Mass, Father Jozo asked the children to come to the rectory for further questioning. He was still not thoroughly convinced the apparitions were heavenly induced. He talked to each one at length delving as best he could into their hearts. Did they consider the possibility that they might be misleading true believers and that to do so would be a sin? He again suggested that it might be better if they had the claimed apparition inside of the church rather than on the hill. It was a difficult session for the priest and the seers.

That evening the hill was again crowded to capacity for the apparition, while the church was empty. The exasperated pastor trudged to the front pews of the church and prayed for guidance.

Monday marked the sixth straight day of apparitions. The visionaries were surprised that the encounters had continued this long, but at the same time they were thrilled. Each of them hoped it would last forever. They wanted the Virgin to give or leave some kind of sign now, thinking that the apparitions would not go on for much longer. The question had been put to the Virgin the evening before: would she please leave some kind of sign because so many people did not believe they were actually seeing her. in response, she simply smiled. [1]

The visionaries were persistent; during the apparition that evening the visionaries again asked the Blessed Virgin for a sign that she was really appearing. The Madonna answered: *My dear angels do not fear. There has been injustice always.* She then added: *My dear angels, there is only one God and only one faith. Let these people firmly believe and they should not fear anything.*

However, an incredible and revealing incident took place that evening. A local doctor from Citluk who had been sent by the authorities to observe the children came forward and asked the seers if she could touch "this heavenly person" they claimed to be seeing. The children asked the Virgin, who then answered: *There have always been unbelieving Judases but let her touch me. She may come closer.*

Doctor Darinka Glamuzina, upon touching where the visionaries said the Blessed Virgin was standing, was instantly fearful and jerked her hand away. She later stated that she felt "something metallic and shocking," sending shivers all through her body. She admitted that she knew then that something was happening there.[2]

The seventh day of the apparitions brought new trouble from the Communist authorities, which inadvertently added to the chance of success of the Gospa's appearances. On this special feast day of

---

1 The request for a sign would mark the beginning of a repeated desire of the visionaries. Eventually, the Virgin would approve and inform them that it would be a permanent sign and thus, the third secret or warning.

2 Several years later Doctor Glamuzina, who had left the Church to become a Communist, returned to her faith and became an open advocate confirming her belief that the Gospa was indeed appearing in Medjugorje. It is stories of individuals like Dr. Glamuzina that helped determine the success of the greatest apparition of modern time.

the Church, the Feast of Saint Peter and Saint Paul, the visionaries were preparing for the Mass when suddenly two official government vehicles, an ambulance and a police car, arrived in the village and came straight to their homes. Once again, they were being taken to Mostar for more examinations.

The children were placed in rooms with dangerous mental patients and the authorities threatened to leave them there until they confessed they were lying. When this did not budge any of them, they were placed in the morgue with dead bodies exposed. The purpose of intimidation however backfired. Nurses and staff gathered around them asking questions and wanting to know more about the Virgin. Some began to cry when told about how they saw her and described her. At the end the chief doctor, an atheist, concluded they were sane and dismissed them, muttering about the wasting of his time with such religious nonsense.

The visionaries returned home; that evening they went to the hill with the largest crowds yet. Meanwhile Father Jozo, unaware that the authorities had taken the children away during the time of the Mass, simply noted mentally that they were not there. If this is truly from God, he thought, why are they not at Mass? He was convinced more interrogation was needed to reach the truth.

It was ironic. The parish priests, including Pastor Jozo, thought the whole thing might be a hoax created by the authorities to continue harassment of the church. The Communist authorities were sure it was the church fomenting insurrection. The result was both bodies of authority wanted the evening gatherings on the hill moved into the church. The priests felt it was the proper setting if the apparitions were real; the Communists were determined to get the people off the hill and into the Church for their "religious nonsense".

Thus, that evening the children asked the Virgin if she would begin appearing to them inside the church. After a noticeable, inexplicable hesitation, she agreed. In hindsight, it put the apparitions where they belonged so that they would lead to adherence to the sacraments of the Church. It would also mark the beginning of mass conversion for the parishioners

Changes far more critical were put into place on the ninth straight day of apparitions. That evening the visionaries told Father Jozo they had something to tell the people before the Mass and he agreed to let them do so. It is Our Lady's desire, they told the assembly, that the people should gather in the church daily to pray a special prayer requested by the Virgin. The special prayer was an old familiar prayer favored by the older women of the village. The people were to pray seven Our Fathers, Hail Marys and Glory Bes, they announced. The creed was to be added at the beginning as they revealed that the Virgin had stated that this was her favorite prayer.

The reaction of the villagers was immediate. They fell to their knees and began praying as requested. A pleased Father Jozo then concelebrated the Holy Mass. He was on fire during his homily. He fervently asked the people, "Are you prepared to *accept fasting* for three days with love, that you restrain yourselves from food so we can resist Satan's attack and drive away the evil that is breaking us apart? Are you prepared every day to *pray in your families* and start reading the Bible?"

The people responded with a loud, yes! They stayed in the church praying until midnight. The spiritual conversion of the villagers of the five hamlets of Medjugorje, so absolutely crucial to its continued success, was defined that evening. The question then was, would it last? The villagers were infamous for family feuds that went far into the past; cursing was common, as was working on Sundays. It would take tremendous, instant changes if it were to survive.

Surprisingly, the initial reaction from the people went beyond the emotion of that incredible evening. Prayer and fasting from that moment became a regular part of daily life for just about every family of Medjugorje. Old family grudges were mended and working on Sundays came to an end; and, cursing, which had been practiced by just about all of the men in the parish, all but disappeared. Now, Father Jozo thought, this is the response needed to unite the parish. Whatever was happening on that hill with the visionaries and villagers might truly be heaven-induced.

The next day brought about the final proof that the enigmatic priest needed to prompt him to become the defender of the visionaries and the strongest promoter of the messages of Medjugorje. As the 10th day of the apparitions dawned, the pastor of Saint James Church went about his business on a busy morning, thinking about what was happening with his flock. In his mind many good things had occurred. He was pleasantly surprised when a large number of parishioners came to the church that afternoon and began to pray fervently for three hours.

However, just before the time of the apparition, the crowd left the church and headed for the hill. Pleasant surprise once again turned into exasperation. Jozo walked to the front pews of the now empty church and prayed fervently. He prayed aloud to the Holy Spirit asking for guidance and discernment. If this is really from God, please, he pleaded, give me a sign. Suddenly Father Jozo heard a clear and distinct male voice: **"Jozo, go out and protect the children!"** Startled, Father Jozo looked around the church. The message was repeated with an additional line: **"Jozo, go out and protect the children and then I will tell you what to do!"**

The stunned priest immediately arose and went quickly to the right side door of the church. As he opened the doors, the visionaries fell into his arms pleading for him to protect them from the police who were chasing them. By instinct, the pastor reacted; he quickly whisked them to the rectory and placed them in a small room[3] before returning to the top step of the entrance of the rectory, He was determined to protect them. Within minutes, the police arrived and brusquely asked, "Have you seen those children?"

With arms folded in a defiant stance, Father Jozo answered firmly: "Yes." Inexplicably, the police did not wait to hear more. Instead, they ran off in another direction.

After the police were out of sight, Father Jozo and the children returned to the church. A short time later, the Virgin appeared in apparition to the young seers, and the priest who had doubted, was convinced that this was really happening to these young people.

From that moment, Father Jozo Zovko believed. Several days later when the visions were finally taking place within the church, he actually saw the Virgin in the choir loft one evening during the time of the apparition to the children. He became the apparition's primary defender. It was a role, which would shortly cost the charismatic priest his freedom.

As the apparitions continued into the month of July, a significant, orderly routine had been put in place. It was needed out of necessity during the chaotic first ten days. The daily apparition

---

3 Ironically, the small room, a bedroom for one of the priests, would become the apparition room later when the bishop forced the Franciscans to move the site of the apparitions out of the church.

was now taking place in the church each evening, just as the priests and the Communist authorities had desired. It was exactly what was needed to bring to fruition the plan of Heaven. Thousands were now coming to pray and be present during this moment of high-powered grace. Many still came out of curiosity and with hopes of having personal prayers answered, but there was no question that the plan of conversion was succeeding.

The evening routine, so vital to the goal of Our Lady to bring her "dear children" as she began to address them, to spiritual conversion, was solidly in place. Every evening at six o clock[4], it began with the prayers of the first two mysteries of the Rosary prayer, the Joyful and Sorrowful mysteries. Usually near the beginning of the third decade of the Sorrowful mysteries (the crowning of thorns), the Blessed Virgin would appear to the six visionaries now ensconced in a small sacristy to the right of the church altar. To the delight of all in attendance, one of the seers would immediately come out and tell them what the Virgin had said to them. Many times it would be little Jakov. The rest of the Rosary would then be prayed followed by Holy Mass.

The newly formed evening routine was not quite finished. Just as the villagers had spontaneously responded in the church at the request of the Virgin on the tenth day of the apparitions, they added the praying of the seven Our Fathers, Hail Marys and Glory bes. The long evening service would then conclude with the praying of the Glorious mysteries. No one in the village would have ever thought they would pray so much at one time! The routine continues

---

4 Five o clock after the daylight savings time change.

to the present time. For Father Jozo, it was as though his prayers had been answered.

There was a severe price to pay by priests, visionaries and villagers alike for their participation in the continuation of the apparitions. Harsh, cruel persecution by the paranoid Communist governing authorities came crashing down on them with the intent of stopping it all.

Would Medjugorje survive and fulfill its plan of salvation for the village, the region and eventually the entire world?

*Especially little children, pray for the gifts of the Holy Spirit so that in the spirit of love every day and in every situation, you may be closer to your fellow man; and that in wisdom and love you may overcome every difficulty. Thank you for having responded to my call.*

—Message given to visionary Marija, May 25 2000.

> "If the world hates you, know that it has hated me before it hated you. If you were of the world, the world would love its own; but because you are not of the world, but I chose you out of the world, therefore the world hates you. Remember the word that I said to you, 'A servant is not greater than his master.' If they persecuted me, they will persecute you. If they kept my word, they will keep yours also."
>
> —John 15:18-20.

## CHAPTER VI: PERSECUTION

NO ONE could have anticipated the severity of government persecution that quickly developed during the first weeks of the Virgin's appearances. As stated earlier, the Communist authorities interpreted the formation of massive crowds on the hill where the Virgin was reportedly appearing as the beginning of a Croatian insurrection. They began plans to crush it before it could grow.

It was a natural train of thought since a predominant number of the ruling Communists were Serbians, ever distrustful of the hated Croatians who made up the majority of the villagers of Medjugorje and the surrounding area. They perceived the massive crowds caused by the apparitions as a direct, treasonous attack against the state. With that in mind, the authorities began to do everything possible to stop the apparitions and punish those directly involved. Their intent was to crush it completely.

A serious meeting took place during the first week of the claimed apparitions in the nearby town of Citluk, involving the municipal and regional authorities. They immediately determined to send informants to the hill each evening when the supposed apparition was taking place. The informants, actually villagers who had joined the Communist Party, would report everything that occurred, including the name of villagers who were regularly present on the hill.

Within days, articles appeared in publications throughout the country denigrating the apparitions as attempts to destroy the Communist regime. Pilgrims coming to the site of the apparition were stopped and bags were searched for hours. Families of the visionaries were harassed and threatened. The visionaries were forcibly taken to Citluk for interrogation, as were several villagers who were attempting to protect the children and bring order to the masses of crowds. The government was sure it could bring the "nonsense" about the appearance of this person called "Our Lady" to a quick end.

Two government authorities were sent to the home of the visionaries with the intent of pressuring the parents. they focused on the mothers, telling them of the consequences their children would face in the future if they continued with their story. They also threatened to take away the passports of the fathers who worked in other countries. Terrified by the threats the young seers hid from the officials to avoid further harassment.

Through it all, the six youths remained steadfast. They stated repeatedly that they had seen and were continuing to see the Virgin each evening. No harassing, lengthy interrogations or threats against them and their families from government authorities could sway them from this claim.

The height of the government harassment came during an important feast day of the Church, the Feast of the Assumption of the Blessed Virgin Mary, celebrated on August 15. The Belgrade government decided it was time to change tactics from harassment and threats to a blunt use of force. It was their way to stop the "subversive movements from the Republic of Bosnia and Hercegovina, called 'Our Lady'".

Special military forces were sent to the area from Sarajevo. The village of Medjugorje was completely surrounded. Armored vehicles full of soldiers patrolled until late at night. Arrests were made for the slightest of things, such as going up the hill at night where the apparitions had occurred. The village was under siege.

August 17, 1981, marked the darkest moment of the 53 consecutive days of apparitions. Early that morning a large force of State Security authorities pulled onto the church grounds near the rectory as the sisters were preparing breakfast for the Franciscans. Members were swarming within minutes inside the rectory and the church. They had come to arrest Father Jozo.

Paranoid fears of the gatherings caused by the daily apparitions remained strong among the government officials. They had warned Father Jozo to stop the evening Mass but he had stood firm in refusing. The plan to stop it was clear: Arrest the leader and it will stop.

The motive the authorities would use for the arrest of the charismatic Father Jozo came from an impassioned homily he had given on July 11. Hundreds had filled the church and grounds to overflowing that evening. The pastor was well aware the authorities were present and recording his every word. He was resigned to the fact that very soon he would be arrested. Several minutes into his prepared words, Father Jozo launched into a fervent passage seemingly aimed right at the Communists. It was the "evidence" they needed to have reason to arrest him and thus, shut down the newly formed evening service of prayers and Holy Mass, which were attracting such massive gatherings.

With eyes flashing, Father Jozo spoke the fateful words: "Jesus came amongst His lost sons and said, 'The Spirit of the Lord is on me, because He has anointed me to preach good news to the poor. He has sent me to proclaim *freedom* for *prisoners* and recovery of sight for the blind, to release the *oppressed*, to proclaim the year of the Lord's favor.' We understand that tonight! Hasn't He come to release me, the *prisoner*, you the *oppressed*, who, for *forty years* have been imprisoned, that tonight or tomorrow, you may kneel down in front of Him and say, 'Open those chains, open those locks, *open the chains that have been tightening my life*, for I have been chained by sins for many years. You are the only one who can do that!'"[1]

It was clear to the Communist authorities. Father Jozo's use of the words *freedom, oppression, prisoner* and, *forty years*, was a direct reference to the 40 years of Communist rule in Yugoslavia. It was obvious in their thinking that these inflamed words gave total proof of treason against the State. When told of his arrest, Father Jozo quietly asked for time to dress. He then calmly left the rectory and was placed in one of the vehicles waiting to take him to one of the most horrible jails in the region to await trial.

The Communists ransacked just about every room in the rectory and the church scattering furniture and items without regard. They confiscated Father Jozo's books and papers, and took money from the collections in the church[2] as well as the recorded tapes of his interviews with the visionaries. Saint James Church was left in shambles, its doors sealed by heavy wooden planks. The villagers

---

1 Excerpt is taken from a copy of Father Jozo's homily that day. Emphasis in italics is added.
2 The collection money was reportedly later returned to the parish.

were in shock and grief. What were they to do now without their church and without their pastor?

While many of the villagers stood around stunned at what was happening, a few brave souls came forward and began to argue with the police that the church was theirs and that they had no right to board it up and prevent them from using it. Another large group kneeled in front of the church's doors and quietly began to pray the rosary. Soon others joined in. It took great courage from all of the villagers present to do this since many of them had already been arrested and placed in jail for far less offenses.

One parishioner who showed calm courage, decided to seek out the chief of the police and boldly ask for the keys to the church. When the chief refused to give him the keys, he calmly said, "It was not you who built this church. We all did that, so give us the keys to our church!"

Surprisingly, the chief reluctantly gave him the keys. Within minutes, a group of women had torn down the planking, which had been nailed to the doors, and the people rushed into their church. The statue of the Blessed Virgin was somewhat tilted from the ransacking of the church by the soldiers. It was quickly restored to an upright position. Soon the church bells were ringing, letting all the faithful know that Mass was about to take place.

Immediately, a volatile situation of confrontation was transformed into a glorious moment for a large multitude of villagers and pilgrims who celebrated the Holy Mass, while the police authorities stood around unhappy but not knowing what to do about it.

The reaction of the villagers to this intrusion of blunt oppression was indicative of the growing influence of the Virgin's visits. Instead of hatred, the villagers offered the soldiers drink and food as they stood guard at designated posts. People went about their day as though all was normal. The invasion only strengthened their resolve to live the messages the Madonna was giving them. At one point, the Virgin told the villagers in a message to the visionaries, *Be kind to the police as well!*

The survival and success of the apparitions, despite such human attacks, depended not only on the grace of Heaven, but foremost on the response of the people. Without the free will acceptance and adherence to the messages, it could not survive. This fact was evident from the very beginning of the apparitions.

An ominous sign of what was to come was given on the first day of Mary's appearance in the village, June 24, 1981. This sign did not come through the Blessed Mother, but from the one who is always at work counteracting her mission: Satan. It occurred suddenly in the early morning hours, as a full-fury summer storm enveloped the valley in minutes, turning the calm of night into unholy terror. Many villagers, startled out of deep sleep by ear-splitting peals of thunder and continuous streaks of lightning, were certain doomsday had arrived. Torrents of hard rain were driven sideways by furious gusts of wind; lightning struck the post office setting it afire. Claps of thunder caused the ground to tremble as though moved by an earthquake. The storm subsided as quickly as it had come, leaving the villagers shaken as they fought the raging fire at the post office.

Only later would these sudden minutes of dark fury be seen as the portentous calling card of the Prince of Darkness, coming to do battle again with the Woman sent by Heaven. Approximately sixteen hours later, in the calm of day, Ivanka first saw the Blessed Virgin on the hillside. Another battle in the age-old clash between good and evil had begun; the new battlefield was the village of Medjugorje.

Two months later, on August 2, in honor of the Church feast day known as Our Lady of the Angels, a strange event took place late in the evening. After the Mass, a small group of villagers gathered with the visionaries in an isolated field away from the church to sing and pray. They wanted to continue celebrating the feast day. The Virgin suddenly appeared without notice to the visionaries. Marija startled the gathering when she announced, "Our Lady says she will allow those who so desire to come and touch her."

As the people rushed forward to "touch" the Virgin, the visionaries would tell them: "You are touching her veil . . . now you are touching her head . . . her dress." Suddenly Marija shouted: "Oh! Our Lady is disappearing and she is completely blackened!" within seconds, the Madonna disappeared.

Marija's neighbor, Marinko Ivankovic, a stalwart defender and protector of the children from the first days of the apparitions, asked Marija what had happened. "Oh, Marinko," she replied, "there were sinners here and as they touched her, her dress got darker and darker until it turned black and she disappeared!"

Marija then asked that all of the people present go to confession the following day. Appalled by this visible evidence of the power of sin, Marinko loudly echoed Marija's call for confession, making sure all were aware of it. This incredible event would set the stage for Medjugorje to become a huge center for the Catholic sacrament of confession. Priests coming to the village on pilgrimage would find themselves spending hours in the confessionals, leading to a renewal of conversion and recommitment for many of them.

Later, in further conversation with Marija, Marinko discovered that another unusual and unannounced apparition had occurred earlier that evening. As Marija was changing into jeans before coming to the field, the Virgin suddenly appeared to her in her room. In contrast to the regular apparition earlier in the day, the Virgin was somber. She said to Marija, *The devil is trying to infiltrate himself here in order to get something. My Son wants to win over all the souls, but the devil is exerting himself to get something. He is making every effort and wants at any price to infiltrate among you!*

"I am not sure if Marija understood Our Lady correctly or not," Marinko was later quoted, "but she stated that Our Lady also said that *she does not know how all of this will turn out* – if the devil will succeed or not . . ."

There is an exact meaning to the Blessed Virgin's warning to Marija during this unexpected extra apparition to her. Of course, it is about the devil wanting to infiltrate among the visionaries and destroy the Medjugorje apparitions as a whole; but there is little doubt that *without the people's response* to her pleadings for prayer, fasting, and penance, the outcome would remain unclear.

The day after this startling meeting in the fields, there were long lines in and around the church for confession, and more the following day. Priests who heard the confessions were astounded at the number and intensity of the confessions. Pleased with the response, the Virgin urged the people through the visionaries to continue on a path of repentance and conversion.

The totality of the harsh reaction against the apparitions was not entirely unexpected from the government. The villagers were used to such tactics against those who continued to practice their faith in the face of atheistic Communism. At the time, it seemed as if things could not possibly be worse than the invasion of government authority. Yet, the people had held their ground, buoyed by the power of the messages the Virgin was giving them through the young visionaries. Without such resolve, the apparitions could have been brought to an end in the first few days.

However, the worse was still to come. No one could have imagined that the local church hierarchy would add to the opposition.

*Dear children, I am continuously among you because, with my endless love, I desire to show you the door of Heaven. I desire to tell you how it is opened: through goodness, mercy, love and peace—through my Son. Therefore, my children, do not waste time on vanities. Only knowledge of the love of my Son can save you. Through that salvific love and the Holy Spirit He chose me and I, together with Him, am choosing you to be apostles of His love and will. My children, great is the responsibility upon you. I desire that by your example you help sinners regain their sight, enrich their poor souls and bring them back into my embrace. Therefore, pray, pray, fast and confess regularly. If receiving my Son in the Eucharist is the center of your life then do not be afraid, you can do everything. I am with you. Every day I pray for the shepherds and I expect the same of you. Because, my children, without their guidance and strengthening through their blessing, you cannot do it. Thank you.*

—given to Mirjana, June 02 2012.

> So in the present case I tell you, keep away from these men and let them alone; for if this plan or this undertaking is of men, it will fail; but if it is of God, you will not be able to overthrow them. You might even be found opposing God!
>
> —Acts 5:38-39.

## CHAPTER VII: OPPOSITION FROM WITHIN

THE CONTRADICTORY move against the apparitions by the highest local leader of the Church marked the beginning of the largest threat posed to its success. They had seemingly endured the ferocious government barrage. Could it now survive an attack from within? The words of the Blessed Virgin spoken to visionary Marija on August 2, echoed in the minds of many: *I do not know how all of this will turn out...*

Bishop Pavao Zanic of the Mostar-Duvno Diocese, which includes Medjugorje, believed so strongly in the apparitions during the early weeks that he visited the parish five times and met several times with Father Jozo at the bishop's residence. The bishop made verbal and written comments stating that such innocent children were incapable of lying about such a thing as apparitions of the Blessed Virgin Mary. In short, he believed they were authentic and said so many times.

When it all started, the bishop was anxious to talk to the visionaries; once arranged, he spoke at length with all of them. He was especially taken by Marija, with whom he quickly developed a warm relationship. On July 1, after a long session with the visionaries at his office in Mostar, Bishop Zanic told Father Jozo, "I am 100 percent sure that it is Gospa who is appearing to these children. I am even more certain of it than of Fatima or Lourdes!"

The Franciscans were cautiously delighted—especially in light of the acrimonious relationship that had existed between the bishop and the Franciscans for years. Could the apparitions be the catalyst for finally bringing about a true reconciliation? It appeared promising during the first two months of the apparitions.

On July 25, the Feast Day of Saint James, patron of the parish, Bishop Zanic came to Medjugorje to administer Confirmation. During his homily, he said, "The public expects us to say something about the events in the parish of Medjugorje where six children like these would have told all in half an hour if anybody had been manipulating them. I assure you that none of the priests has done any such thing. Furthermore, I am convinced the children are not lying. They are saying only what they profoundly believe."

The bishop and the Franciscans were solidly working together in defense of the apparitions against the government's attempt to stop them. It could not have been more ideal. However, within the next few weeks, the goodwill between them came to an abrupt halt.

It began in early August when Bishop Zanic asked Father Jozo to come see him about an urgent matter. Pressure was being applied to the bishop in heavy doses by the government authorities to end the apparitions, he told the pastor. Of course, the same pressure was being applied to Father Jozo, who had been ordered to stop the evening services; he had refused, knowing and accepting that his arrest was simply a matter of time.

Father Jozo was so exhausted from lack of sleep that he asked another priest to drive him to the bishop's residence in Mostar. Once there, Bishop Zanic took him by the hand away from the others present to a nearby window and said to him, "Father, today I have been summoned to come to Sarajevo. They told me that if I protected Medjugorje, if I still stood by Medjugorje, they would lock me up." The bishop grabbed Father Jozo's arm and added, "I cannot go to prison for Medjugorje. I am a bishop!" Father Jozo was left dumbfounded. He did not know how to reply.

Adding to the bishop's fear, several days later, a hastily assembled anti-Medjugorje group of 12 priests, which included two Franciscans, came from Rome to meet with the bishop. They threatened him that if he continued his support of the apparitions, they would "chase him out of the diocese". Now he was facing pressure from the government and from this group of priests from Rome to denounce the apparitions, even though they did not have formal authority.

Once again, Bishop Zanic called Father Jozo to his residence in Mostar. How, he asked the priest, could he not comply with the demands of the 12 priests? "I cannot go back to being a village chaplain, can I?" he said. "In your opinion, can I, a bishop, become a country curate (priest)?"[1]

It is clear from these two meetings with Father Jozo that Bishop Zanic was more concerned about keeping his position as bishop than about complying with the truth he knew in his heart. From his earlier comments in the first weeks of the apparitions, he was certain

---

1 The information about the meetings between Father Jozo and Bishop Zanic is taken from the book **Encounters With Father Jozo**, by Sabrina Covic, published in 2003. It is the only authorized book about Father Jozo that he has allowed to be published. The statements attributed to the bishop and Father Jozo are exactly as given by Father Jozo, according to the book.

the Mother of God was appearing in apparition in Medjugorje. He knew it and he stated it verbally and in writing. However, unlike Father Jozo, he seemingly was not willing to sacrifice his position as bishop for the truth. It is the only feasible conclusion that appears to explain such reaction to threats from the government and the anti-Medjugorje priests.

Father Jozo never told of the urgent meetings with Bishop Zanic until he testified before an investigating commission, one of two commissions, which had been organized under orders from the bishop. Bishop Zanic also testified at the commission, and with Jozo present, was asked if the comments given by Father Jozo were true. He stated that he "did not remember".

Even after such a statement, Father Jozo did not hold any anger or resentment against the bishop. He would later state during an interview, "Neither then nor now do I hold it against him. I do not attack him, nor do I judge him."

Shortly after this second meeting with Father Jozo, Bishop Zanic was presented with a way out of the dilemma. It came through an answer from the Blessed Virgin during one of her apparitions by way of a response to a question by a Franciscan priest put to her through one of the visionaries. Surprisingly, she answered the question and the answer gave the bishop a reason to abandon his support for the apparitions.

A look at the past and immediate history of the acrimony between the bishop and the Franciscans is necessary to understand how an answer to a question put to the Blessed Virgin could affect the bishop's position in defending Medjugorje. In short, it was a case of humanity over holiness in the form of church politics, wrapped in human jealousy over the love of the Franciscans by the people of the parishes. The control of parishes in the diocese of Mostar-Duvno was the crux of the problem that went back nearly a century.

Priests of the Franciscan Order had been serving in the region for more than 400 years prior to the invasion and subsequent 400-year rule by the Turks, which began in the fifteenth century. The invasion also brought the influence of Islam into the region. The Franciscans, an order of Catholic priests formally organized to follow the example and teachings of Saint Francis of Assisi, kept the Christian faith alive through underground methods during this period. Because of this, they were overwhelmingly beloved by the people.

The secular priests—diocesan priests with no affiliation to a specific religious order—were introduced into the region in the late 1880s. It immediately caused problems for the laity. They were only familiar with the Franciscans and did not want the diocesan priests; they wanted their beloved Franciscans. It created numerous rebellions by the laity against the newly installed secular priests in the parishes. Of course, the Franciscans were accused by the secular priests of being behind the rebellions.

The problem continued into the twentieth century. When Pavao Zanic, a secular priest was appointed as bishop of the Mostar-Duvno Diocese in September 1980, he immediately began a program of changing many parishes by installing secular priests in place of Franciscans. In May 1981, Bishop Zanic disciplined two Franciscan friars by defrocking them,[2] because they had conducted Masses for the people in the Franciscan chapels in Mostar. This was

---

2 An act of removing the faculties of an ordained priest to administer the sacraments of the Church.

in direct violation to his orders that the people attend Mass only in the Diocesan cathedral in Mostar.

Thus, when the apparitions began in Medjugorje, a Franciscan priest asked visionary Vicka to put the question to the Virgin if the discipline of the two young Franciscans by the bishop was justified. The answer surprised all concerned. The Gospa told Vicka that in the matter of the bishop defrocking the two Franciscan priests, the bishop had acted hastily and should reconsider his decision. When the bishop was told what the Madonna said by Vicka—likely in a more blunt and direct way than Our Lady had given it—he puffed up in consternation and said, "The Blessed Virgin would never speak to a bishop this way!"

Bishop Pavao Zanic now had a reason and a way to separate himself from defense and involvement in the apparitions. The termination of support would keep him out of jail and allow him to remain a bishop. He immediately denounced the apparitions as false, claiming the visionaries were lying; the Franciscans were manipulating them and making up the messages; and, it was a grand scheme for them to make money and gain power for their order.

From that moment, Bishop Zanic became the major opponent of the apparitions, a position he maintained until his retirement from the office in July 1993, and to his death in January 2000. He went out of his way to justify his denouncement of the apparitions. However, he never explained his zealous support of them in the first two and a half months. The acrimony between the bishop's office and the Franciscans reactivated and the immediate result was a stronger polarization between secular priests and Franciscans.

In the ensuing years, two different commissions were formed by Bishop Zanic to investigate and rule on the authenticity of the apparitions; both were packed with carefully handpicked members who were known for their biased negative stance on Medjugorje. It was at the first of these two commissions that Father Jozo was asked to testify and then told about his August 1981 meetings with Bishop Zanic.

Little investigation was done by the negative members of either commission. Only one member actually went to Medjugorje to see firsthand what was happening. As expected, both commissions ruled that the apparitions were not supernatural.

The biased ruling by both commissions was not ignored by the Vatican. In a surprising step, It overruled both commissions and then made an unprecedented move by taking the authority of investigating the apparitions completely out of the hands of Bishop Zanic. The authority was then placed with the Conference of the Bishops of Yugoslavia. It remained with them until the civil war disrupted the entire region, which soon saw the end of the Federation of Yugoslavia and the reestablished governments of the six republics that comprised the former state.

On April 10, 1991, just two months before the spreading of the civil war, the Bishops' Conference of former Yugoslavia issued the "Declaration of the Ex-Yugoslavia Bishops' Conference on Medjugorje, which stated,"The declaration makes clear that while at that particular point in the investigation, "it cannot be affirmed that one is dealing with supernatural apparitions and revelations", it went on to say, "one *cannot* be affirmed that it is *not* dealing with supernatural apparitions and revelations". In short, it cannot be affirmed it is supernatural or not supernatural. This very important declaration went on to state: "the faithful journeying to Medjugorje, prompted both by motives of belief as well as other motives require attention and pastoral care."[3]

The Declaration neither approved nor condemned the apparitions, but did permit *personal belief* in the apparitions and *personal pilgrimages* to Medjugorje while the Church investigation continued. Therefore, neither a parish priest nor a bishop could organize a church-sponsored official pilgrimage to Medjugorje, but any individual—including priests and nuns—could *unofficially* go as private citizens. It is, in essence, the standing position of the Church in all past and present reported apparitions until confirmed or condemned by an investigative body of the Church.

The stance by the Church has remained the same since the last issuance of the Bishop's Conference in August 1993, which stated, "We bishops, after a three-year-long commission study accept Medjugorje as a holy place, as a shrine. This means that we have nothing against it if someone venerates the Mother of God in a manner also in agreement with the teaching and belief of the Church... Therefore, we are leaving that to further study. The Church does not hurry."[4]

I was present in Medjugorje in July 1987, when Bishop Zanic came to the parish for Confirmation. To the dismay of the parishioners, he used the occasion to denounce the apparitions, taking away the joyful celebration from the young people being confirmed into the Church. I did not need a translator to understand what was happening. The visage on the face of the local pastor of Saint James Church, Tomislav Pervan, was total frustration; the predominant reaction of the villagers bordered on pure anger.

---

3 *Declaration of the Ex-Yugoslavia Bishops' Conference on Medjugorje,* Ex-Yugoslavia Conference of Catholic Bishops, Zadar, April 10, 1991.
4 Published in the regional church magazine, Glas Koncila, August 15, 1993.

In fairness, it should be known that Bishop Pavao Zanic was a devout man with a strong veneration of the Blessed Virgin Mary. He unquestionably believed in the apparitions of Lourdes and Fatima. The bishop's favorable position on the apparitions in the early days inspired and gave courage to other church leaders who, for whatever reason, had not yet taken a positive stance towards them. That included Father Jozo Zovko and the other Franciscans stationed at the parish of St. James when it all began.

I remember a story visionary Marija related to me concerning Bishop Zanic, whom she remained fond of even after his change of stance. She told me that a couple of years after the start of the apparitions, she convinced the other visionaries to come with her to Mostar to visit Bishop Zanic on his birthday. They arrived at the entrance of the bishop's residence and rang the bell. When Bishop Zanic answered, they joyfully sang happy birthday to him. He stood there looking dour and afterward said to Marija, "I know why you are doing this; you want me to change my position and believe in the apparitions!"

Marija shook her head negatively and embraced him saying, "No, bishop. We do this because we love you!" He then softened and invited them in where they spent time with him without further mention of the subject that so divided them.

The inclusion of the history of Bishop Zanic and his early support and then denouncement of the apparitions is essential to the whole of the story of Medjugorje. It is more so with his successor,

Bishop Ratko Peric. Sadly, opposition to the apparitions would continue with greater fury when he took office in July 1993.

Father Ratko Peric was widely recognized within the diocese as the protégé and eventual successor to Bishop Zanic. He was extremely upset with the bishop's early belief and active support of the apparitions. I learned from a reliable source close to the situation that Father Peric aggressively warned Bishop Zanic not to get involved with "this business of claimed apparitions" and the Franciscans who were, in his estimation, "behind it all." The century-long feud between secular and Franciscan priest strongly affected him.

However, there is a critical fact relevant and revealing about Bishop Ratko Peric and his rigid negative stance on the apparitions. It is that Bishop Peric *does not believe in any apparition* of the Blessed Virgin Mary—past or present. This belief is the foundation for his opposition to the apparitions at Medjugorje, along with the stated history of antagonism between Franciscans and secular priests infamously titled the "Hercegovina Affair". There is no reason to delve further into this confusing and polarizing situation. Despite tepid claims from individuals on both sides that the feud is long forgotten, it remains an underlying issue and strong contributing factor in opposition to the apparitions by Bishop Peric.

Things in Medjugorje immediately began to change for the worse under the authority of the new bishop. During the next six years, he used every occasion possible to attack the authenticity of the apparitions. He wrote to the parish priests of Medjugorje, reminding them of a series of restrictions he imposed:

  ✠   The priests were not to identify the site of the alleged apparitions as a "shrine";

⅋ They were not to promote events connected with the apparitions, and not to include the visionaries in formal parish activities;

⅋ The prayers and messages connected with the alleged apparitions were not to be printed in the parish bulletin, nor used in parish prayer services;

⅋ The local and visiting priests were not to comment publically (during homilies) on the messages;

⅋ Visiting priests who came to Medjugorje from outside the diocese were not to hold conferences or retreats without the bishop's permission;

⅋ Any priest who visited the parish was required to provide proof that he had proper faculties from his own bishop before celebrating Mass there.

Many of the bishop's stipulations were in line with standard Church practice concerning apparitions; but his purpose was not based on seeing to proper procedures concerning the apparitions. His purpose was to shut down all mention of them and attempt to restrict the normal activities of the Franciscans and the visionaries that had become part of the evening prayer service. He went far beyond the purpose of the practices and wrongly included restrictions against the young seers. In fairness, the apparitions and stories about them were used frequently by visiting priests during homilies in Saint James Church. The Franciscans as a whole promoted the events in commentaries to visiting pilgrims and in written works.

In July 2006, as the parish celebrated 25 years of the ongoing apparitions of the Blessed Mother, Bishop Ratko Peric did the same thing his predecessor Bishop Zanic had done in July 1982. He used the occasion of the Confirmation at Saint James Parish in

Medjugorje to serve as a platform to rail against the apparitions. In a homily given during the ceremonies and later posted on his diocesan website, Bishop Peric stated: "Brothers and sisters, let us not act as if these 'apparitions' were recognized and worthy of faith. If, as Catholics, devoted sons and daughters of the Church, we want to live according to the norms and the teaching of the Church, glorifying the Holy Trinity, venerating Blessed Mary ... and professing all the Church has established in the creed, we do not turn to certain alternative 'apparitions' or 'messages' to which the Church has not attributed any supernatural character."

Again, the villagers were shocked and angry. The bishop continued his assault: "As the local bishop, I maintain that regarding the events of Medjugorje, on the basis of the investigations and experience gained thus far throughout these last 25 years, the Church has not confirmed a single apparition as authentically being the Madonna,"

The bishop was correct. The Church had not confirmed a single apparition at Medjugorje as being authentic. Of course, what he failed to mention or acknowledge was the fact that canon law of the Church states that no claimed apparition can be verified or approved while it is apparently still in progress.

Continuing the dubious "tradition" started by his predecessor, Bishop Peric used the confirmation services at Medjugorje in 2008 once more as an opportunity to denounce the apparitions. During his homily he said, "Therefore, I responsibly call upon those who claim themselves to be 'seers', as well as those persons behind the 'messages', to demonstrate ecclesiastical obedience and to cease with these public manifestations and messages in this parish. In this fashion, they shall show their necessary adherence to the Church, by neither placing private 'apparitions' nor private sayings before the official position of the Church!"

The villagers wondered how Bishop Peric could repeat a second time an act of such unkindness to the young people being confirmed. It becomes more questionable in light of the statements of the Ex-Yugoslav Bishop's Commission in August 1993. Further mystifying is the fact that Bishop Peric *never* conducted a personal or official investigation of the apparitions taking place so close to Mostar. He has *never* spoken with or interviewed the visionaries; and, he visits Medjugorje only rarely for Confirmations and official functions.

As stated previously, there is no desire or agenda to denigrate the person or the office of Bishop Ratko Peric. Like his predecessor, he has a strong love and devotion of the Blessed Virgin Mary, even though he does not believe in any Marian apparition. He is well known in the region and state for his leadership qualities and has given generously of his time and material goods in many local causes. All of which leaves one wondering how such staggering spiritual evidence of good fruits pouring out of Medjugorje could be so overlooked by the leader of the local church hierarchy.

The mission to destroy the "cult of the apparitions" as the bishop viewed Medjugorje was revved up to full throttle in the summer of 2009. The bishop issued new regulations in which the visionaries could not have their alleged apparitions on any church property. Long-standing lay religious formational groups were told they had no formal permission to be in Medjugorje as supposed religious organizations. No church-owned property could serve as a site of an alleged apparition. Like the government in the early days, the bishop went from harassment to strong action, using every possible avenue afforded by his office as bishop.

However, Bishop Peric and his assault on the veracity of the apparitions was stopped shortly after the private, unofficial visit to Medjugorje by Cardinal Christoff Schönborn of Vienna in December 2009 (chapter 14). The Cardinal's subsequent meeting with the Pope, and then the formation of the Vatican commission in March 2010, finally led to silencing Bishop Peric, who a few months later, stated that he would reserve judgment (and comment) on the apparitions until the commission made a formal statement. Other than a couple of outbursts over trivial matters, Bishop Peric kept his word—until May 2012.

Imagine the shock of the villagers and worldwide followers of the apparitions when Bishop Peric made a bizarre statement during confirmation services at Medjugorje on May 20. He said to the people of the village, "You have the opportunity to make a Jerusalem of this parish, a site of action of the Spirit of God, where there is the unity among a multitude of peoples, where everyone understands everyone in God, not in the fake wealth, where the word of Peter is being heard: 'Repent … and receive the gift of the Holy Spirit'."

Bishop Peric was referring to the booming growth of new hotels, large expansion of private homes to house pilgrims, restaurants, condominiums, shopping malls, clothing stores and huge department stores springing up all over the community. He pointedly singled out those villagers chasing the lure of riches and power by attempting to build more and sell more. He was right. The grace of the apparitions that seemingly enveloped every villager in the early days of the apparitions was fading into the background of many villagers for the opportunity to get rich quick.

I have witnessed first-hand the evil of greed and deceit amongst an alarming number of villagers—especially the younger ones who have grown up in a radically different culture than their parents of the early days of the apparitions. In the first twenty years, there were few shops and amenities. Coming to Medjugorje on pilgrimage was meant to be a religious experience away from worldly ways.

Now, I see tour agencies using comfort and convenience as major selling tools to get people to come on pilgrimage. New hotels and expanding homes with pilgrim rooms now include internet access and televisions in the rooms. Many have air conditioning and central heating. The major concern seems to be how much money can be made.

Fortunately, there are still many local business owners and tour agencies who remain devoted to the spiritual call of the apparitions. This is evident by the packed services each evening, especially on the weekends when the faithful from the surrounding communities come to Medjugorje.

The bishop was clearly stating in his confirmation homily that Medjugorje had an important choice to make. It could be a "New Jerusalem"—a place of holiness; or, if consumed by the recent boom in commercialism, it could fall into spiritual ruin and become the next "Babylon"[5]. The statement left followers wondering. Was the bishop finally coming to believe in the apparitions? It certainly sounded as though he did. Alternatively, was he apprehensive of the Vatican commission's final report, which according to well-founded rumors would be released sometime in 2013? A third factor is also

---

5 Revelation 18:1-3 identifies the city of Babylon, chief city of ancient Mesopotamia and capital of the kingdom of Babylonia, as follows: And he called out with a mighty voice, "Fallen, fallen is Babylon the great! It has become a dwelling place of demons, a haunt of every foul spirit, a haunt of every foul and hateful bird; for all nations have drunk the wine of her impure passion, and the kings of the earth have committed fornication. with her, and the merchants of the earth have grown rich with the wealth of her wantonness."

conceivable. Possibly, the bishop was concerned that following release of the commission's report, a new diocese would be formed, which would incorporate as its centerpiece the parish of Medjugorje, taking it out from under his rigid 19-year history of opposition.

The hope of the parish and the world-wide followers of the Medjugorje apparitions is that Bishop Ratko Peric may have finally realized because of the overwhelming good fruits, that the Mother of God truly is appearing daily in the village. Only time will tell.

I emphasize again that it is imperative to include all of the facts and information concerning the negative position and actions of Bishop Pavao Zanic and his successor, Ratko Peric. There is no intent to disrespect or unfairly judge either man or his position as a bishop of the Catholic Church. However, as individuals both are responsible for personal actions.

Following in the wake of the harsh government attack on the apparitions, the actions of both bishops stood as another stiff trial for acceptance and success of the apparitions. After 31-plus years of daily apparitions—and counting—it is fair to state that the good fruits continue to overshadow the bad.

It has taken exceeding courage by individuals and various groups to keep the grace of the messages of the Medjugorje apparitions flowing. Without the acceptance and positive response of the villagers in the early days, it would not have continued. If people did not come from around the world on pilgrimage to see for themselves and experience spiritual conversation, the good fruits would have been modest; and, without the accounts by individuals through books and other media on what was happening there, it might have been just another interesting footnote in the history of Marian apparitions.

The greatest courage in keeping the apparitions on the right track was shown by the "shepherds" as the Blessed Virgin calls her beloved priests. There were many. However, one brave Franciscan priest deserves special recognition as the one most responsible for its continuation and success as a place of spiritual conversion—Father Slavko Barbaric.

*Dear children! My motherly heart suffers tremendously as I look at my children who persistently put what is human before what is of God, at my children who, despite everything that surrounds them and despite all the signs that are sent to them, think that they can walk without my Son. They cannot! They are walking to eternal perdition. That is why I am gathering you, who are ready to open your heart to me, you who are ready to be apostles of my love, to help me; so that by living God's love you may be an example to those who do not know it. May fasting and prayer give you strength in that, and I bless you with my motherly blessing in the name of the Father, and of the Son, and of the Holy Spirit. Thank you.*

—Message given to visionary Mirjana on March 2, 2011.

> The Lord has sworn and will not change this mind. "You are a priest forever after the order of Melchizedek."
>
> —Psalms 110:4.

## CHAPTER VIII: SLAVKO, THE LEAD SHEPHERD

MANY PRIESTS played important roles in the early days of the Medjugorje apparitions. It was essential that the messages purportedly coming from the Blessed Virgin Mary were authentic apparitions and not of a demonic nature. To assure they were completely in line with Church doctrine and Holy Scripture, the local priests had to display strong leadership in discerning and implementing proper practices and responses to the specific requests of the messages. If Medjugorje's apparitions were going to change the world, they would have to be carefully studied so as not to mislead the public.

Two "shepherds" stand out above the others for their early leadership in Medjugorje: Jozo Zovko and Slavko Barbaric. Without their efforts individually and jointly, Medjugorje may not have survived to become arguably and unofficially, the most important Marian apparition in the history of the Roman Catholic Church. Of the two, Father Slavko emerged as the "Lead Shepherd of Medjugorje".

The unofficial title of lead shepherd takes nothing away from the accomplishments of Father Jozo and the other priests involved with the apparitions over the years. It includes those in the parish as well as all who came from all over the world. The term "shepherd" is one that the Blessed Virgin uses frequently to describe the priests. It is a term of affection; and, it clearly is meant to make the faithful of *all faiths* aware of the role and responsibility church leaders have in leading their flocks.

Both Bishops of the Mostar-Duvno Diocese, who served during the time of the apparitions, targeted Father Slavko and Father Jozo as the ones most responsible for promoting and prolonging the apparitions. Father Slavko received the bulk of their collective ire because of the length of time he was there to direct proceedings.

Father Jozo took charge early to assure that the response was based on the sacraments of the Church. He courageously defended the visionaries and established an order of worship to keep the flock faithful. Knowing the consequences of standing up to the persecuting Communist authorities, he was determined to protect them and the villagers. For those actions, he was arrested by the government and placed in jail, where he would serve a sentence of 18 months at hard labor.

There was no one among the Franciscans at Medjugorje to take up the jailed pastor's leadership role as defender of the apparitions. It happened so swiftly. Father Tomislav Vlasic was appointed pastor in the interim and did his best to maintain order until he was transferred out of the area. That brought the leadership as pastor to the studious Father Tomislav Pervan, who established a calm maintenance.

The well-educated Father Slavko would come on to the scene when he was initially asked to investigate the apparitions by Bishop Zanic in 1983, primarily to confirm the bishop's stance that they were not authentic. Father Slavko was selected for this assignment because of his earlier work at Medjugorje as a psychotherapist. He had studied and analyzed the visionaries for several months. His work with the seers during that time was completely objective. Therefore, the bishop figured he was the right choice to judge what was happening. He was a Franciscan priest with esteemed theological credentials and two doctorates. Surely, this educated man would come to the same negative conclusion as the bishop; he would straighten out his fellow Franciscans and convince them to give up this charade.

The exact opposite of what Bishop Zanic had hoped for happened. After weeks of observation and study, Father Slavko calmly reported to the bishop that he found the apparitions to be authentic. It was the consistent flow of good fruits coming from the daily apparitions, which served as a basis for his belief—not science or psychology. Such obvious evidence went far beyond the theological and psychological teachings he had mastered in his years of higher education. Bishop Zanic was furious. He was convinced that Father Slavko had joined Jozo Zovko as a co-conspirator in the Medjugorje debacle.

From the time of his birth in March 1946, Slavko Barbaric seemed destined to be a Franciscan priest. In hindsight, it could be stated that he was also destined to be the pillar of spiritual strength that would keep the Medjugorje apparitions on the necessary spiritual path desired by Heaven.

Slavko's family, though extremely poor, lived in faith to God. He served as an altar boy from an early age. By the time he reached the eighth year of school, 15-year-old Slavko determined his call to become a Franciscan priest. Blessed with a strong intellect, he studied philosophy and theology, both of which would lead to his earning two doctorate degrees that would serve him well later at Medjugorje. Slavko learned languages with ease, especially German, which became a favorite. The ability to learn languages would also be a valuable tool at Medjugorje. He was fluent in seven European languages including English.

In addition to studies and duties as a newly ordained priest, Father Slavko worked tirelessly in helping others regardless of their faith or lack thereof. However, it was his work with youth that most pleased him. He formed a youth encounter group at the parish of Siroki Brijeg in 1972, which grew over the years from a few hundred attendees to more than 10,000 annually. It was the honing of his talents and experiences working with young people that would form the framework of many of his programs at Medjugorje. One of them was the annual Youth Festival. It started in the summer of 1989 when a few hundred young people gathered in Medjugorje for spiritual inspiration stemming from the Gospa's messages. The seemingly tireless priest stepped forward to organize the beginnings of the movement. It quickly grew from a small number to more than 80,000 by 2012, which marked its 23rd consecutive year of occurrence.

It was more than youth programs that gave Father Slavko the unofficial title as the leader and defender of the Medjugorje apparitions. He became the architect and founder of the many spiritual programs at Medjugorje that are so popular today. If it were not for his leadership, spiritual guidance, public witnessing through talks in numerous countries as well as a plethora of writings, the apparitions may have accomplished far less. Its defense and spiritual development became the learned Franciscan's passion, but in a quiet, matter-of-fact way. To him, what was happening daily in the village was clearly a grace from God and the proof was in the growing numbers of pilgrims coming there and returning home with a true spiritual conversion.

I met Father Slavko in June 1986, during my second pilgrimage to Medjugorje. At that time, he had two extremely difficult responsibilities involving the apparitions as well as a growing multitude of other tasks. The first responsibility was to oversee and translate literally word for word the monthly messages meant for the faithful received by visionary Marija on the 25th day of each month. It was critical to assure that every word of every message complied with Holy Scripture and Church doctrine. His second and more daunting task was to oversee each evening's apparition and determine who would be allowed in the room during the time of the apparition.

The apparition room was a small bedroom-office located in the front of the rectory. Huge crowds of pilgrims gathered on the grounds outside of the rectory each evening prior to the time of the apparition. Many of the pilgrims in the crowd were ill with major illnesses or conditions and had been brought there by family members. All of them wanted to be with the visionaries when the Blessed Virgin Mary would appear, hoping for the miraculous cure. However, there was room for only about 35 people in the tiny room.

Father Slavko always made sure that visiting journalists were given an opportunity to be in the room along with priests and scientists. Next were the terminally ill and those with life-threatening conditions. If there were spaces left after satisfying these groups, others would be allowed in by random choice. Each evening brought about gut-wrenching emotional confrontations and hard decisions. It took a group of local village men to maintain order among the anxious pilgrims.

In addition to these responsibilities, Father Slavko also counseled young people struggling with drug addiction. His work with addicts would later grow with the establishment of a special rehabilitation center at Medjugorje called Cenacolo, started by an Italian nun named Sister Elvira. Father Slavko became the spiritual guide for the center's inhabitants. It was through one of his early patients that I met him. She was a 16-year-old Australian girl who was recovering from a drug addiction who was half-Croatian from her mother's side and spoke the language fluently.

"What are you writing?" I heard someone ask early one morning in June 1986. I was back in the village for my second visit, working with a portable typewriter on a small wooden bench in front of the rectory. Startled to hear someone speaking English since there were virtually no English-speaking pilgrims in Medjugorje at the time, I looked up to see a blond teenager perched at the other end of the bench. I told her that I was awaiting a meeting with one of the priests and that I was working on some notes. I barely finished my sentence before she blurted out, "My name's Tanya – what's yours?"

Within minutes, I knew Tanya's full story of drug addiction. I was beguiled by her non-stop stream of conversation intermingled with questions about my work and why I was in Medjugorje. Tanya had been in the village for nearly two months under the psychological and spiritual care of Father Slavko. It had been arranged by her mother as a last-ditch effort to save her life. She had just overdosed for the seventh time.

Over the next several days, Tanya would seek me out for conversation and company, which was appreciated by me as there were only a few people there who spoke English; soon I was doing the best I could to give her good advice and point out how fortunate she was to be under the care of Father Slavko. She caught up with me one afternoon as I walked the church grounds and immediately said, "He wants to meet you—I told him you were a journalist."

Two days later, I was sitting in Slavko's office, the small room that presently served as the apparition room—and his bedroom when in Medjugorje. I was awed to be in this special place and even more to be able to meet and interview the intense, thin-faced theologian who also served as spiritual guide to the visionaries. Tanya was there as translator at his request.

There was another purpose for Father Slavko to meet me; he wanted to assure that my intentions in befriending his young charge were on a proper level.

I began the interview by asking the charismatic priest about his first days with the visionaries. He said that almost immediately after meeting and questioning them, he was sure they were without guile. If that was the case, then the apparitions were indeed occurring just as they described. He added that he felt a special burden for the spiritual life of each of them.

When asked why these children, Father Slavko paused a moment and then quoted the message the Blessed Virgin had given to the visionaries when they asked the same question: "I do not always choose the best people."

"That may sound harsh," Father Slavko added through Tanya's translation, "But the fact that Gospa purposely chooses ordinary people gives unquestionable credibility to such phenomena." He went on to explain how difficult to imagine anyone suspecting such simple children of perpetuating a hoax of such magnitude for five years daily. Somewhere in that time, the relentless probing of teams of scientific, medical and canonical investigators would have uncovered it. For that reason, he added, he always gave journalists, clergy and scientific teams first consideration in deciding who should be present during the apparition.

There was another important point Father Slavko covered. I asked him, why children? Why would the Virgin not choose adults or, more explicitly, priests and/or professionals in medical and scientific fields rather than children? Would that not give automatic credence? "No, not necessarily," he answered. "By appearing to young, uneducated and unsophisticated children, the Madonna leaves room for pure, blind faith."

Listening to this priest so gifted with a sense of simple common sense was a treat. I was learning far more about the visionaries and Medjugorje in general than I had in all of the books I had read before coming on pilgrimage. We went on with the interview for nearly an hour. Tanya was superb as a translator. Father Slavko was also pleased with her and let her know it.

The meeting changed course after I had exhausted my questions; now, I was the one being interviewed. Father Slavko wanted to know my story and how it involved Medjugorje—and of course, my new friendship with Tanya. I told him my story of conversion and about my work as a journalist. Finally, after answering his questions, I ended the meeting, even though reluctant to do so.

Thanking Father Slavko for his time, I got up and prepared to leave. However, Tanya excitedly motioned for me to stay and then whispered into the priest's ear. "Oh, yes," he said smiling—now suddenly speaking in fluent English, "Please come to the rectory this evening to be present when Gospa comes. You need to be here in order to report it accurately."

I immediately realized Slavko had allowed Tanya to serve as translator even though it was not necessary. He had done so simply to give her another opportunity to build self-esteem. However, the importance of his invitation was not overlooked—as a journalist and as an individual. I stood there nodding numbly and thanking him, too overwhelmed to say more.

That evening marked my first time of being in the apparition room. I witnessed the heart-breaking pleas from so many who wanted into the room—and I felt guilty. I was there simply because I was a journalist. I knelt next to visionary Marija, mesmerized to be so close to someone receiving messages from the Virgin. Young visionary Jakov was also present. Father Slavko motioned for him to pray a decade of the rosary as we awaited the arrival of the Virgin, which he did in a loud, clear voice. Upon finishing, he looked at his spiritual director for approval. Slavko simply motioned for him to do another. With a pained look of resignation, he complied.

Moments later, the prayers stopped in mid-sentence; the Madonna was appearing to the two visionaries. Two men from an unidentified scientific team got up and lifted Jakov approximately three feet off the floor, while a third filmed the incident. He remained in a state of ecstasy with his knees bent in prayer, as if he were a statue. After approximately four minutes, it was over. Soon I was outside of the rectory after thanking Father Slavko profusely.

The experience of being present for an apparition left me literally speechless for some time afterward. The entire episode with Tanya and the ensuing interview she arranged for me with Slavko marked the beginning of a tremendous friendship with him. We always met for a chat when I journeyed to Medjugorje after that. I would also see him frequently at conferences in the United States, where both of us were invited as speakers. We were able to share many hours in conversation and I came to appreciate the value of his friendship and incredible talents, as a priest and as an individual.

Tanya would remain in contact sporadically over the years even though she would struggle mightily to overcome her drug addiction. The good news is she finally did. One important reason for her eventual success was that Father Slavko never forgot her and stayed in touch to assist her whenever possible.

Slavko knew from the time of his first encounter with Medjugorje that it was his special calling as a priest. He was there to monitor it to assure it was the work of Heaven and to defend it from all attacks. It seemed that the Blessed Virgin had arranged for this special priest to be there. She would soon confirm it when, according to visionary Ivan, he received a special message from the Gospa on February 3, 1985. The Virgin said, *"I wish Slavko to remain here and attend to all details and the notes so that at the end of my visit, we will have a synoptic image of everything. I am praying especially for Slavko at this time and for all those who work in the parish."*

Having already served in Medjugorje for two years, the confirming message from the Blessed Virgin Mary cemented his intent to stay there despite the many attempts of Bishop Zanic, and later Bishop Peric, to have him transferred away from the parish. This was to be his mission. It would also become a cross through his constant clashes with the presiding bishop.

From the early work of Father Jozo Zovko in establishing the evening routine of prayer and Holy Mass, as well as being a special spiritual guide to the visionaries, Father Slavko expanded it to include multiple programs and projects. All of them adhered to the call of the Virgin's messages. Medjugorje was, as he called it, a huge school of conversion, a school of love and peace. It was demanding, he said, but the teacher was the Mother of God. Her curriculum was prayer, fasting and penance. Homework included regular attendance at Holy Mass, confession at least once a month and daily praying of the Holy Rosary. Her chosen head shepherd would do everything in his power to see to its fulfillment, sure of the Virgin's words directed at him in the message given to visionary Ivan.

In that span of time, the tireless priest founded a much-needed orphanage called Mother's Village, which stands today as possibly his crowning achievement. It came about because of the horrible civil war that raged in former Yugoslavia from 1991 well into 1995. Hundreds of thousands of innocent people were killed and many more became refugees. Father Slavko wanted the orphanage to take care of the little ones who lost their parents in the evil conflict. It continues today as a special place, which now also includes a home for drug addicts.

During his 17-plus years of service in Medjugorje, Father Slavko was constantly in conflict with the local bishop, who for unknown reasons could not see the work of extremely good fruits taking place in the parish. This was especially true with Bishop Peric. He ordered the moving of the charismatic priest to distant parishes several times, hoping this would keep him out of Medjugorje. It did not work. Slavko was always present in the parish to maintain the daily programs, no matter the distance from his assigned parish. The struggle continued right up to his unexpected death.

In November 2000, Bishop Peric was sure he was finally going to be rid of Slavko Barbaric by transferring him to a mission site away from Medjugorje. He hoped it would be the last order to remove the stubborn priest from the village for good. Usually, Father Slavko would find a way around the transfers and always show up in the village to continue his work—after taking care of daily duties at his assigned parish. This time, there seemed no easy way out.

Bishop Peric was determined to stop the Medjugorje problem, as he saw it, and that meant getting rid of the head shepherd, Slavko. He started in early 2000 by ordering his priestly faculty to hear confessions removed—not only in Medjugorje, but also throughout all of the dioceses of the Hercegovina region. Father Slavko told me about it when we met in the summer of 2000 during the youth festival. I will never forget his look of resigned vexation as he told me, "He took away my ability to hear confessions for no reason …"

The bishop was not done. He later threatened to remove all of Slavko's faculties as a priest if he did not obey and accept the transfer—and stay away from Medjugorje. Father Slavko was desperate and appealed through his provincial to the Vatican in Rome. There was no concrete reason to remove him from Medjugorje other than the desire of the bishop in his quest to stop all events surrounding the apparition site. He was accused by the bishop of being disobedient and he struggled with the dilemma of being obedient to the bishop versus the calling to spread the good news messages coming out of the village.

I returned to Medjugorje in early November 2000 and, of course, looked forward to seeing Father Slavko. However, he was hard pressed for time, as though determined to accomplish as much as possible before having to comply with the new orders from the bishop. We did not have time for our usual informal chat; fortunately, I ran into him one morning on the east side of the church. He walked up to me and gently patted the side of my face, smiling and asked, "How are you, how is your family? Are you still speaking on the messages?"

"Yes, I am still busy traveling to spread the word," I answered, grateful for the few minutes with him. Little did I know it would be the last time I would see or speak to my beloved friend.

On Friday, November 24 2000, the last day on earth for the head shepherd of Medjugorje, it was not clear if his appeal to Rome would be successful so that he could stay in the parish. As far as Bishop Peric was concerned, the trouble-making priest would leave Medjugorje for good on Monday, November 27. However, it was not to be.

On Friday afternoon, Slavko led the usual crowd of parishioners and pilgrims up the steep, rocky path of Krizevac Mountain, something he had been doing for years. At the top, he spoke to the crowd for a few minutes, led the group in prayer and proceeded to make his way back down the mountain. Suddenly after going approximately fifty feet, he stopped and slowly lowered himself on a rock. Seconds later, Father Slavko collapsed. He was dead within minutes.

Over the next two days, thousands of people passed by his coffin in respect for the Head Shepherd of Medjugorje. He was laid out in the Adoration Chapel located to the left and below the formal church grounds. It was a fitting place as he was the one who had introduced adoration of the Holy Eucharist to the parish.

On Sunday afternoon, November 26, Slavko Barbaric, OFM, only 54 years old, was buried in the cemetery behind the church. His life was celebrated at a requiem Mass before the burial. Ironically, the service was presided over by Bishop Peric. For the 120 or more priests on the outside altar of Saint James Church as well as thousands in attendance, no one worried about the bishop's presence. It was not a time of resentment or anger. This was a time to rejoice even though grief-stricken.

There was motivation for such joy by the priests, the villagers, the visionaries and the millions of Medjugorje followers throughout the world. It came from the precious words spoken by the Blessed Virgin Mary as she gave the monthly message to visionary Marija on November 25, the day after Slavko's death. She included a special mention of him by adding at the end of the message: *I rejoice with you and I desire to tell you that your brother Slavko has been born into Heaven and intercedes for you!*

It was clear to all of the followers of the apparitions that the work of the Lead Shepherd of Medjugorje would continue.

*Dear children! Today when Heaven is near to you in a special way, I call you to prayer so that through prayer you place God in the first place. Little children, today I am near you and I bless each of you with my motherly blessing so that you have the strength and love for all the people you meet in your earthly life and that you can give God's love. I rejoice with you and I desire to tell you that your brother Slavko*

*has been born into Heaven and intercedes for you. Thank you for having responded to my call.*

—Monthly message given to visionary Marija on November 25, 2000.

> The point is this: he who sows sparingly will also reap sparingly, and
> he who sows bountifully will also reap bountifully.
>
> —2 Corinthians 9:6.

## CHAPTER IX: JOZO AND THE OTHER SHEPHERDS

FATHER SLAVKO BARBARIC was not alone in his support, defense and organizing of the Medjugorje apparitions. It was far too huge a task for one individual. Several brave priests made valuable contributions during its formative years just as critical to its success. They, too, had to face the consequences of going against the persecution by the government officials trying to shut the apparitions down.

The leadership of Father Jozo Zovko deserves special credit. As stated earlier, he played the initial role in organizing and maintaining the spiritual events that developed from the apparitions during the early days. This brave priest did so in the face of threats from the government, which would soon lead to his arrest. He was tried for treason against the state and given a three-year sentence at hard labor in one of the worst prisons in the region. The devout priest's response was to humbly accept his fate and then proceed to evangelize his fellow inmates.

It soon became clear to the young Medjugorje seers that their pastor was a special instrument of Heaven's plan through the apparitions. On August 17, the day of his arrest, when the visionaries and the villagers were filled with grief and worry, the Blessed Virgin assured them through a message to the visionaries that Jozo was under her protection: *Do not be afraid. I wish that you would be filled with joy and that the joy could be seen on your face. I will protect Father Jozo.*

Again, on August 22: *Father Jozo has nothing to fear. All troubles will pass.*

The Virgin clarified how critical a part Father Jozo played in the apparitions on August 28. They had been waiting for her to appear to them at the usual evening time, doing so in Father Jozo's room at the rectory, the same room in which he had placed them in the early days of the apparitions to protect them from the pursuing police. They prayed fervently but Gospa did not come. It was only the second time it had happened.

Disappointed and sad, the seers decided to go to the church and pray. Gospa appeared to them as they prayed, bringing them joy—and relief that she was still appearing to them. She explained, *I was with Father Jozo. That is why I did not come. Do not trouble yourselves if I do not come. It suffices then to pray.*

The Blessed Mother also related why she did not appear to them in Father Jozo's room, telling them that someone had placed (hidden) listening devices in the room. She added: *The world is on the point of receiving great favors from me and my Son. May the world keep a strong confidence.*

The words of the Virgin at this time served as a powerful confirmation that the messages and events at Medjugorje were meant for the entire world. For the visionaries, it was also assurance that their spiritual advisor was safe and covered by the mantle of the Blessed Virgin.

There definitely was reason for the visionaries and villagers to worry about Father Jozo. Surviving the treatment of his government antagonists at the time of his arrest was dangerous and extremely difficult. The arresting party barged into the rectory and ordered him to get ready. He knew what they meant and began donning his Franciscan habit when he was brusquely stopped and ordered to dress in civilian clothes. He could take nothing with him; no habit, cross, Bible—no religious items.

The pastor of Saint James was placed in a small police car and quickly taken away. Just outside of the village, the car stopped and Father Jozo was told to get out. As he did so, his captors moved away from him. He noticed a large number of militia encircling the small area with guns pointed at him. Jozo understood immediately; they wanted him to attempt an escape so they could shoot him. When the prisoner did not move, he was roughly led to a large black van and thrown in the back on the floor where he could not see where he was being taken.

Father Jozo was placed in the jail at Mostar, where he was sharply interrogated as they tried to force him to admit he was a traitor to the state. Charges were screamed at him that he was inciting war, hatred and the overthrow of the government. He was given no food or water and was physically abused numerous times during the ordeal as guards took turns provoking him. Jozo's only response to his tormentors was to state repeatedly, "I speak only for Jesus—nothing else interests me!"

A tiny shaft of light penetrated the darkness of what was happening to Father Jozo during these several weeks of torture and interrogation. He was not allowed to read anything and knew nothing of what was occurring at Medjugorje since his arrest. A guard who was opening the door one evening to place Jozo back into the cell whispered to him, "My mother has been on pilgrimage to Medjugorje." At that moment, the beleaguered priest was overjoyed and knew that everything was continuing on a spiritual path in the village. Several years later, Father Jozo would baptize this guard.

Another noteworthy incident occurred after what seemed endless days of interrogation of Jozo. Like so many Croatian men, he was a heavy smoker. They took his cigarettes from him during his arrest and did not allow him to smoke during the days of interrogation. Later, a guard, possibly feeling a little sympathy for the Franciscan, flipped a pack towards him, telling him to go ahead and take it. Father Jozo stared at the pack of cigarettes for a moment before calmly pushing it away and saying to the guard, "No thank you, I don't smoke." From that moment, he decided to quit the habit. He has never smoked since.

After the trial and sentencing, Jozo was placed in one of the worst prisons in the area. It was filled with murderers and thieves. He survived the initial harassment, physical abuse and threats from fellow inmates by being passive, quoting Scripture and sincerely listening to the few men who came to him for guidance. Before long, word spread that a Franciscan priest was imprisoned with them. Soon, many fellow prisoners were coming to him.

Ironically, Jozo was fulfilling a mission of evangelizing to prisoners, something he had always wanted to accomplish but had not been allowed.

Strange things began to happen in the prison. Prisoners and guards alike claimed that they could see an aura around the priest. He had a charismatic way of speaking and comforting those who came to him. Strangest of all, once Father Jozo was locked in his cell, the lights would be turned off; yet, there was always light there. Then as soon as the guards walked away, the cell door would open. It would be relocked and it would open again. This continued for a time until finally, the guards, thoroughly shaken and frightened, accepted that it was useless to attempt to lock this holy priest in his cell. On August 30, 1981, the Blessed Virgin Mary confirmed the "little miracle" when visionary Vicka asked if it was true that Jozo's cell door could not be locked. She answered, *Praise be Jesus! It is true, but no one believes it.*

Father Jozo was 40 years old when he was arrested and placed in prison. His early life was similar in numerous ways to that of Father Slavko Barbaric. He was born in a small village near Siroki Brijeg, about 25 miles from Medjugorje. Jozo was one of ten children. Like Slavko, he knew at an early age that he wanted to become a Franciscan priest. The 1945 infamous slaughter by the Communists of a large number of Franciscans at the parish of Siroki Brijeg—where he would later serve as pastor—gave inspiration to him. He saw his ordeal at the prison as insignificant to that of the martyred Franciscans. He knew he would survive.

Jozo did survive prison. His sentence was eventually reduced to 18 months from the original three years. He was released on February 17, 1983, but in a final show of disrespect, the prison kept him an additional 12 hours claiming clerical work to be responsible for the delay.

The newly freed priest did not want anyone to come for him. He took public transportation (bus) to Sarajevo and on to a small suburb of Mostar, where his sister Fabijana lived. As the bus arrived, the road was full of nuns and friars there to welcome him home.

Within a short time, Father Jozo was celebrating his first Mass since his arrest.

When Jozo returned to Medjugorje, he was told he had been transferred to another parish. It was difficult for him to accept this. He loved Medjugorje. However, he discovered that he could take Medjugorje with him regardless of his assignment or the level of ongoing harassment against him. He did not argue but went to the newly assigned parish.

Several days after arriving, the police summoned him to a meeting, where he was informed he could not carry out his priestly duties in the new parish because he was a political convict. Jozo refused to accept the conditions. He was quickly reminded that he had to submit to whatever was asked of him. Jozo paused and then responded, "I have not yet unpacked my suitcase. I can just as well return to the prison, but I will not spend my life and my priesthood at half strength. On the contrary, I want to work, I want to give everything because I have received everything!"

The police were helpless to argue with the fact that Jozo would not obey their orders. They had no choice but to let him go, adding a final shot: "You will be transferred anyway!"

In a few days, Father Jozo was transferred to an extremely poor parish in Bukovica. It was in this parish where the harassed Franciscan began his predestined mission: to work with youth and to preach the word of God, using the experience of Medjugorje as the foundation. Medjugorje pilgrims started coming to the little parish to hear him speak.

In 1985, Jozo was transferred to another parish called Tihaljina. Pilgrims followed in even larger numbers. I learned later that an Italian man named Dino Lunetti organized the first waves of pilgrims to come to listen to Father Jozo. It marked the beginning of an integral part of all pilgrimages to Medjugorje. Pilgrim groups from all nations would go to hear him speak and have him pray over them. Several years later, Dino's son Paolo would marry visionary Marija. Visiting pilgrims also discovered a special statue of the Blessed Virgin Mary in the church at Tihaljina. It was breathtakingly beautiful and seemed to be alive. Father Jozo began distributing a picture of the face of the statue to the visiting pilgrims. It would eventually become the "face" of the Virgin Mary at Medjugorje. Within a few months, thousands of pilgrims were coming to Tihaljina to see and hear the famous priest—and to see the statue of the Blessed Virgin.

It did not take long for the local bishop Paolo Zanic to turn against his former confidant whom he had confided in during the government's threats to jail him. The reason the bishop gave was Father Jozo's constant "promotion" of the apparitions. He soon stripped him of his faculties, just as Slavko had been stripped of his. When Ratko Peric became bishop, he continued to harass him, still thinking of him as a perpetrator and inventor of the apparitions.

No one defined the general message the Blessed Virgin continues to give to the world as clearly as Father Jozo did during his talks. This alone gives reason to see him as a special instrument in bringing the apparitions to success by invoking the sacraments of the Church as its foundation. Miraculous healings occurred when he prayed over pilgrims. Spiritual conversions numbered in the thousands among those who went to hear him. Today, he is stationed far from Medjugorje in the city of Zagreb. He is not allowed to speak about Medjugorje or of the messages, a penance, which now serves as his cross.

Regardless of the persecutions, whether from the government or from the local hierarchy of the Church, Father Jozo continues to be a tenured part of the apparitions to the villagers, the visionaries and to all of the visiting pilgrims. Like Slavko, he became a personal friend and we visited often when in Medjugorje. I see him as a true living saint—which is exactly what Our Lady of Medjugorje called him during the early days of his government oppression.

Other shepherds served valiantly at Medjugorje. Father Tomislav Vlasic served in Father Jozo's place briefly as pastor of Saint James Parish after Jozo was arrested. He helped the visionaries as spiritual guide and generally worked tirelessly to maintain the programs started by Jozo. Unfortunately, he later became involved in a cult-like movement, which eventually led to his personal request for laicization by the Catholic Church. It was granted in 2009. All of these events happened well after Tomislav Vlasic left Medjugorje.

Many opponents of the apparitions at Medjugorje quickly condemned the apparitions, pointing to the human failures of Tomislav Vlasic as evidence that they were false or a hoax. However, Father Tomislav left Medjugorje in 1984, shortly after being relieved of his duties as pastor. He was never involved with the apparitions or the visionaries in a spiritual capacity after that time.

Father Tomislav Pervan followed Father Vlasic as pastor of Saint James Parish, assuming the position in 1984. A quiet learned man, he possibly had the toughest job of all, sustaining the progress and growth of the good fruits. It was his responsibility to keep the parish focused during the tumultuous times of the surging growth of

Medjugorje as a place of pilgrimage. Father Tomislav also faced the constant opposition of Bishop Zanic. He handled it all with humility and hard work.

Lastly, Father Svetozar Kraljevac, also stationed at Medjugorje during the beginnings of the apparitions, contributed as a spiritual director to the visionaries. He authored one of the first books on the apparitions, which influenced me more than any other book. I was blessed to work with him on other writings, while he would turn the tables and assist me in writing my first book. He unselfishly traveled throughout the United States during the civil strife in former Yugoslavia gathering large donations to assist the refugees.

Father "Svet", as the followers of Medjugorje know him, is presently in charge of Mother's Village and has been since the death of his beloved fellow Franciscan, Slavko. He is a frequent speaker at Medjugorje to the visiting pilgrim groups.

The shepherds of Medjugorje continue to care for the flock, which takes in all who have traveled to Medjugorje as a pilgrim. The list of shepherds is not limited to the Franciscans stationed in and around Medjugorje; it includes every visiting priest, preacher and minister who has heard the call to come to Medjugorje. Without their leadership in pastoral care, Medjugorje would have failed as an apparition site.

It comes down to realizing that if the focus were only on the sensationalism of a supernatural event, and not on the tremendous grace as a gift from God, the opponents of the apparitions would have triumphed. The major opponent, Satan, would have succeeded in crushing it from the beginning.

Now, let us see who these young people are who were chosen to be visionaries and messengers of the Blessed Virgin's words.

*Dear children! With motherly love I implore you to give me your hands, permit me to lead you. I, as a mother, desire to save you from restlessness, despair and eternal exile. My Son, by His death on the Cross, showed how much He loves you; He sacrificed Himself for your sake and the sake of your sins. Do not keep rejecting His sacrifice and do not keep renewing His sufferings with your sins. Do not keep shutting the doors of Heaven to yourselves. My children, do not waste time. Nothing is more important than unity in my Son. I will help you because the Heavenly Father is sending me so that, together, we can show the way of grace and salvation to all those who do not know Him. Do not be hard hearted. Have confidence in me and adore my Son. My children, you cannot be without the shepherds. May they be in your prayers every day. Thank you.*

—Message given to visionary Mirjana May 2, 2012.

> "And it shall come to pass afterward, that I will pour out my spirit on all flesh; your sons and your daughters shall prophesy, your old men shall dream dreams, and your young men shall see visions..."
>
> —Joel 2:28.

## CHAPTER X: A SPECIAL ROLE FOR MIRJANA

THERE IS no question that all of the Medjugorje visionaries are equal in their role as Gospa's special messengers. Yet, singular focus on Mirjana is warranted due to the unprecedented double part she has been given. She was the first to stop having the daily apparitions, which occurred in December 1982. Five years later, the Gospa revived her role by first coming to her through inner locution, which later changed to a once-a-month active apparition. In addition, Mirjana is the seer chosen to reveal the ten secrets when that time comes

In the beginning of the revived apparition, which occurs on the second day of the month, the seer was not allowed to disclose them for the public. That changed in the latter part of 1997 when the Virgin informed Mirjana that it could be held publicly in the presence of visiting pilgrims. It has continued until the present and remains a major attraction of the ongoing phenomena.

The reemergence of Mirjana as an active visionary, albeit only once a month, is unprecedented in the history of Marian apparitions. For that reason alone, she deserves special recognition and separation from the other visionaries in reviewing her participation as one of Gospa's messengers.

Living in the city of Sarajevo at the time when the initial daily apparitions began, Mirjana was the "outsider" even though she had been born in Medjugorje. Pretty, blond, and outgoing, she became the early unofficial spokesperson for the visionaries, assuming the position without premeditated intent. As such, she was the main target for accusations of perpetrating a hoax by government authorities and some of the local priests. The unfounded accusations quickly died down with the consistency of her story, as well as the intelligence noticeable as she related what had happened in the beginning days.

Mirjana lived and attended school in Sarajevo, coming to Medjugorje in the summers to stay with her grandparents. She was very much the typical teenager, her head filled with things of the world. By her own admission, she paid little attention to spirituality and attended church more out of habit than desire. Personal prayer was rare for her. The bright young woman had planned for a career in agronomy after attending the university in Sarajevo. All plans changed after the initial week of apparitions.

The most difficult period came when the new Medjugorje visionary returned to Sarajevo to continue her schooling. Word quickly spread about the Medjugorje apparitions and that she was one of the so-called visionaries. Mirjana was taunted by students and teachers alike and constantly threatened by the Communist authorities, who came almost daily to harass her. Before long, she was expelled from her secondary school, one of the best in the country. The expulsion was just one more way to harass her by the authorities. The shaken Mirjana was forced to attend an inferior school filled with delinquent youth who had been ousted from the better schools because of behavior.

The young seer remained steadfast in her newfound spirituality, and why not when the Mother of God was appearing and speaking to her daily. It was difficult being separated from the other visionaries, who at least had each other for moral support as they went through similar struggles. Mirjana visited Medjugorje as often as she could, always returning for the summers. Yet, she would have to return to the place of constant harassment to finish her schooling. She remained steadfast and survived it all.

A mind-boggling occurance happened to Mirjana on February 14, 1982, while she was attending school in Sarajevo. It was unlike any personal experience of the other visionaries. Instead of seeing the Blessed Mother on this day, Satan appeared to her.

Mirjana nearly blacked out and later said, "I felt as if I was sinking through the surface. Everything was black and it seemed to be happening from a distance, as I could hear an echo. I heard him offer me beauty and success only if I renounce God and Our Lady. He asked me to follow him and he would make me happy, that I only suffer because of Gospa. I am still uncertain whether I really shouted or the voice was coming from my soul, but I kept saying no, no, no! Suddenly Satan disappeared and the Blessed Mother came. I instantly felt as if nothing had happened at all. She gave me additional strength and said, *My dear child, forgive me for what you had to experience, but you need to know that Satan exists.* She also said that we live in a time of Satan and it had to be that way. She admired my faith."

Mirjana would later add that Satan is very offensive and active at this time, destroying marriages, making priests and ministers doubt their calling, possessing people and even murdering some. She said Our Lady tells us to protect ourselves through prayer, fasting and always carrying religious objects on our person and having them in our homes.

On July 18, 1985, the Virgin gave this message: ***Dear children, today I call you to place more blessed objects in your homes and that everyone should wear a blessed object on his person. Bless all objects, thus Satan will attack you less because you will have armor against him...***

As time went by, each visionary was randomly receiving the ten secrets of future events promised by the Blessed Virgin. They were given to the seers individually without advance notice and in no specific order. In late December 1982, Mirjana, who had received nine of the ten secrets, the first of the six to do so, was told by the Madonna that the following day would be her last time to receive the daily visits. It was December 24, 1982. The Blessed Mother appeared to her as usual and gently told her, ***On Christmas I will appear to you for the last time.*** Mirjana was devastated even though she knew it was coming. How could she survive without the daily visit from her Spiritual Mother?

On Christmas, the young seer was given the tenth secret, a very grave one she later reported. The Virgin had stated in the early days that once a visionary received all ten secrets, she would no longer appear to them daily. She also promised that she would appear to them at least once a year for the remainder of their lives. For Mirjana, that appearance would be on March 18, which happened to be her birthday.[1]

---

1 Mirjana would make it clear in later interviews that the Virgin did not choose this date because of her birthday, but for other reasons that would be known only when the apparitions were over.

During the final apparition, the Gospa appeared to Mirjana for more than 45 minutes. Afterwards, she said that she would always remember the words of Our Lady on that day: *Now you will have to turn to God in the faith like any other person. I will appear to you on the day of your birthday and when you will experience difficulties in life. Mirjana, I have chosen you; I have confided in you everything that is essential. I have shown you many terrible things. You must now bear it all with courage. Think of me and think of the tears I must shed for that. You must remain courageous. You have quickly grasped the messages. You must also understand now that I have to go away. Be courageous.*

Mirjana confirmed later that Our Lady prepared her for this meeting for a month. In a motherly manner, the Virgin had explained that her task was accomplished and she had received sufficient information. She was now free to continue her education.

Regardless of the preparation, Mirjana was distraught. The young visionary felt that her conversations with Our Lady were so necessary for her soul and she did not know how she would go on. However, the Virgin promised that as long as Mirjana remained close to God, she would be there to assist her in the most difficult moments. For the present, she must return to the normal everyday life of young girls her age.

In a later interview with a priest, the first visionary to receive the 10 secrets explained what Our Lady meant when she said she would also appear at times of difficulty: "Father, I am not speaking of the ordinary problems of my life. My difficult moments stem from the secrets concerning the future of the world, which Our Lady revealed to me. At times, I can hardly cope with it when I seriously think of it. In those moments, Our Lady appears and gives me strength and courage to go on with my life."

The final meeting left the young seer feeling as if she had lost the most beautiful thing in her life. True to the Blessed Virgin's warning, the first month after this last apparition was most difficult. Mirjana experienced depression, avoided people, and shut herself in her room where she normally had the apparition. She cried and called out to her, and, as a true mother feeling sympathy for her daughter, the Gospa allowed her to feel her presence. All Mirjana could do now was to wait for her birthday so that she could see her beautiful Virgin again.

There was encouraging news for Mirjana when Mary told the other visionaries that she would no longer be appearing to her. It came a week later on January 1, 1983, when one of the other seers asked the Blessed Mother if she was no longer appearing to Mirjana. The Virgin said, *After Christmas, I am no longer appearing to her for the present.* It is the last three words of this message, "for the present", that set the stage for an unprecedented occurrence in Marian apparition history. Never has a chosen visionary been brought back as an active visionary once told that her visits were over.

As promised by the Mother of Jesus, Mirjana began having inner locutions[2] on August 2, 1987. The locutions would gradually strengthen over time into a full once-a-month apparition. The transition would take nearly 10 years and were just for Mirjana and her family. Meanwhile the annual apparition on March 18 continued.

---

2  An inner locution occurs when a person hears and/or sees the Blessed Virgin Mary interiorly, rather than in the traditional three dimensional view of a visionary. There are varying degrees of hearing; the highest is where one hears verbally as opposed to hearing "with the heart."

Mirjana grew much more mature in her inner life as well as in her character with a strengthened resolve to live the messages and directions she had received in her 18 months as recipient of daily visits from Heaven. In September 1989, she married Marco Soldo, the nephew of Father Slavko Barbaric. They settled into daily life in the village, continuing a long tradition of simple living and focus on God. Eventually, two beautiful daughters were born.

As the inner locutions continued, the entire family would awaken early on the second day of the month and begin prayers as Mirjana waited to hear the inner presence of the Virgin Mary. Some days, the Gospa would come early, while on others, it would take hours. With the new apparitions, the Virgin stressed the renewal of the original focus given to her —to pray  for unbelievers.

In October 1997, Gospa gave rejuvenated seer the first message she was allowed to share with the public. It has continued to the present. There is no doubt of the focus to pray for unbelievers as is seen in the tone of the second-of-the-month messages. The messages are strong and blunt. While they are meant especially for the unbelievers, the Blessed Mother stressed they are also for everyone.

I have been privileged to meet and interview most of the visionaries, and eventually to develop a close relationship with them. It is a blessing to know them personally, but it makes interviewing them somewhat difficult. An interview I did with Mirjana several years ago—more of a general chat than a formal interview—is memorable for many reasons, but mostly, for giving a glimpse of the human side of the visionaries.

During our talk, I tried to ask questions based on inquiries I had heard over the years. Here is a small segment of our talk with another good Medjugorje friend, English-speaking guide Slavenka

Jelevic, serving as translator. Mirjana speaks English very well but prefers the translation in order to give the clearest answer.

During a November 2012 pilgrimage to Medjugorje, our group was blessed to have a private audience with Mirjana and Vicka. The talk and questions following it were basically the same I have heard since my involvement with the apparitions. Thus, the informal interview listed here is essentially the same as that with Mirjana in November.

Here is a portion of that interview:

W: The apparitions have been going on for a long time. Did you ever think in the beginning that they would last this long?

M: **I had never heard about Lourdes or Fatima before, so when I read a book about Lourdes, I read that Our Lady had appeared 17 times or something like that--** (I interrupted and told her it was 18 times) **-- okay, 18 times, and I thought the apparitions would last that long in Medjugorje.**

W: Do you think that the time of the apparitions here has been extended because it is working, because it is touching so many people?

M: **No, it has its own time. When I read about Lourdes and then it continued after 18 times, I said it would last long.**

W: I look at Medjugorje's apparitions as the most important event occurring in the world today. Do you also see it that way?

M:  **It is the most important event in God's life! Through Medjugorje, God shows us how much He loves us.**

W:  I ask this because at the end of the apparitions in Medjugorje, Our Lady says she will never appear in apparition on earth again, that this will be the conclusion of all apparitions.

M:  **She has never said** (to me) **never again on earth. Of course, this is my personal opinion that Our Lady meant that she has been appearing a long time to us six visionaries in this way in common and that this would never happen again.** (Comment: two other visionaries, Vicka and Marija have confirmed that the Virgin said she will never again appear in apparition on earth. Thus, Mirjana is saying that the Virgin did not tell her this as directly as she did the others.)

W:  You gave a statement to Fr. Tomislav Vlasic (former pastor at St. James Parish and one time spiritual guide to the visionaries) in November 1982, which was a summation of the Medjugorje messages, which he put into a letter to Pope John Paul II. In that letter, Our Lady seems very serious about what she was giving here in Medjugorje. This is why I see Medjugorje as the most important event in the world today. Do you remember this letter?

M:  **Not really. In these first years, I have given so many statements to the priests! We were questioned all the time.**

W:  In this statement you stated that Satan had appeared to you disguised as the Blessed Virgin Mary –

M: (interrupting me) **I don't want to talk about that.**

W: Okay, I just wanted to ask if this stills happens to you.

M: **When I talk about Our Lady, I do not want to talk about him. He has always been standing under her heel and he has that much strength** (as) **we give him. And, if God and Our Lady are in the first place in our life, he cannot do anything. If you don't have problems in your work, you must ask yourself if you are working for God. Because, I always think if everything is coming easy, am I working for God? Working for God, you must know you will always have crosses.**

W: You have your own prayer life and that with your family. What about fasting, which seems to be the hardest part for people to live the messages. I know it's difficult for me, and maybe difficult for everyone. Do you literally have fasting in your family, with your husband, with your children?

M: **Yes, of course, even before the apparitions we had fasting in our family on Fridays. This is to teach something and we must learn from that. What can God ask from me if I cannot fast?**

W: What about when you have family problems, do you have a more stringent fast, such as just water?

M: **For me in the beginning I fasted on bread and water, but I would eat too much bread and would feel my stomach was too full but I would still be hungry. Now I fast on just water, because this is** easier for me, maybe some small piece of bread later. I know from speaking to American groups, it is hard for them to fast. I can recommend to them to maybe have some fruit or a little vegetable or something like that.

W: Yes, I agree. They are always asking me if they can have butter on the bread or drink juices and coffee or eat other things besides bread and water.

M: **People must understand that this is a gift, something you want to do from the heart.**

W: This is a little different question. Bishop Ratko Peric of Mostar has opposed the apparitions from the beginning and does not believe they are real. Have you ever personally had an opportunity to sit down with the bishop and talk about Medjugorje?

M: **No, I never have. He has never asked to talk to us but if he asked to talk to us, I would go immediately to him.**

W: Mirjana, you were the first to receive all ten secrets that will occur in the world after the apparitions conclude. You stated that Gospa told you then that she would no longer appear to you daily but would come to you once a year on March 18, which is your birthday. Does she come on this day because it is your birthday or is there some other reason for this day?

M: **It's funny to me when people say that she comes on my birthday, so then I think they do not understand that with Our lady,** there are no privileged children. I am the same to her like you are. So, as much as my birthday is important, yours is also important (to her). Our Lady does not appear on this chosen day because it is my birthday. She has never said to me 'happy birthday!' so when the feast starts (that is, the end of the apparitions) then we will understand why she chose 18th of March, and why she chose to appear to me again on the second day of each month.

W:  She appeared to you until December 1982. Then she began to appear to you on the second day of each month. Did you know this would happen, that she would appear to you at this later date in apparition again?

M:  I knew when she came on December 25 1982 that I would not get the daily apparitions anymore. She said the apparitions on the 18th of March would last my lifetime. And then also, she said that I would have extraordinary apparitions. These apparitions started on the second day of August 1987. So, these are normal apparitions and during the apparition we pray for those who did not learn or need (that is, seek) God's love yet. This is my mission to pray for those who do not feel God's love and I really do not know how long these apparitions on the second day of each month will last. (Comment: as of this writing, they continue to occur on the second day of each month. It has become the biggest attraction in Medjugorje with massive numbers of pilgrims coming to the village to be there for this apparition.)

W: Are the messages you receive from Our Lady on the second day of the month different in any way from the messages you received when you were seeing her on a daily basis?

M: **All these messages Our Lady is giving are about Jesus and they are no different.**

W: I have noticed a difference in the messages you receive on March 18, from the other ones. They are more blunt and direct. They seem stronger.

M: **I think the ones on the second** (day of each month) **for me are stronger. Because when I look into the face of the Blessed Mother, she is more determined, more direct.**

W: Do you read the monthly messages that Marija receives?

M: **No, because when I receive the message on the second of the month, I see the face of the Blessed Mother, and I don't see them** (the monthly messages) **in the same way you do. I see the expression of her face and the way she feels. The messages she gives to Marija are more gentle, like to little children, where the messages she gives to me are for bigger children, you know, adults.**

W: You mentioned earlier the date August 2, 1987. That was the day in August 1981, which was the feast day of Our Lady of the Angels, that people first saw the miracle of the sun. It is also the day when you and Marija were with some of the young people who were in the prayer group and Our Lady appeared again and told you that she would allow them to touch her. Is that date, that incident, the reason why Our Lady chose to begin appearing to you again on the second day of each month?

M: **No. Many beautiful things happened on this day. You will understand later why this day is the day she chose to appear to me.** (Comment: The point she was making is that we would understand, after the apparitions were concluded and the secrets began happening, why this particular day was chosen. And, not only this day but the other days such as March 18, when Our Lady appears to her annually.)

W: You take in pilgrims here at your home. Is this your only source of income?

M: **No, my husband also works and earns income for us.**

W: The last thing I want to ask you about is other visionaries, other locutionists. I know you have met many who come here and tell you they have the same gift of being a visionary or locutionist. Do you ever feel anything special about them, or can you tell if they are real?

M: (Mirjana laughs) **Oh, yes, many have come and told me these things. But no, I don't feel anything special about them when I am with them. I simply tell them when they claim this to pray, to really pray about it. Ask God to explain to you why and what He wants from you. Only my prayers help me to understand what**

**God wants from me through Medjugorje. And of course, you can only judge on the good fruits that come from such experiences.**

W. Thank you, Mirjana.

There was one question I put to Mirjana during our November 2012 meeting: Does a priest from the parish check the messages you receive on the second day of the month for errors? Mirjana answered, "I report the messages just as they are given to me. They are then translated and sent out to the public." Not satisfied with her response, I asked her translator Miki Musa if he could give me further clarification. It was an important point to clarify that each message is checked for adherence to Church doctrine and Holy Scripture. Miki, whom I have known for many years, told me that yes, a priest checks the messages for any errors and for accuracy in the translation.

There was much more given during this interview. However, listening to her answers and comments gave solid proof of her last statement; that is, you can only judge by the fruits that come from such events.

To further confirm why I single Mirjana out from the other visionaries, she is the singular visionary chosen by Gospa to release the information about each secret just before it is to occur. This, in itself, is a tremendous responsibility. Mirjana will do this by choosing a priest who will fast and pray for seven days, announce to the public that the secret will be made public in three days; and, then release its contents by whatever pubic communication(s) he wishes. The priest selected by Mirjana, Father Petar Ljubicic, is now stationed in Medjugorje at Saint James Church.

As stated, each visionary is asked by the Blessed Mother to pray for a specific intention. For Mirjana, it is to pray for unbelievers. A closer look at the other seers solidifies that each has a definite part in the fulfillment of the last Marian apparitions on earth.

*Dear children with motherly love, today I call you to be a lighthouse to all souls who wander in the darkness of ignorance of God's love. That you may shine all the brighter and draw all the more souls, do not permit the untruths which come out of your mouth to silence your conscience. Be perfect. I am leading you with my motherly hand – a hand of love. Thank you.*

—Message given to Mirjana on February 02, 2010.

> But as for you, continue in what you have learned and have firmly believed, knowing from whom you learned it and how from childhood you have been acquainted with the sacred writings which are able to instruct you for salvation through faith in Christ Jesus.
>
> —2 Timothy 3:14-15.

## CHAPTER XI: THE OTHER MESSENGERS

THREE of the youth chosen to become visionaries were close friends before the apparitions. Vicka, Ivanka and Mirjana were nearly inseparable. While they knew the others, they had little in common with them other than school and the close proximity of their homes. That changed on June 24, 1981, when the Madonna made her first appearance in the village.

The visionaries selected by the Blessed Virgin were ordinary teenagers not much different from most young people of the same age. Life before the apparitions consisted mainly of daily chores and school. They were not overly pious or terribly bad. In fact, there was no visible outstanding trait that would qualify them over others in the village to be chosen for such a grace. They were, as visionary Mirjana would later describe, "neither good nor bad, just like everyone else."

Each seer is noticeably different in temperament and personality, adding to the authenticity of the event as each described their initial apparition with minor differences. How could six youngsters, four girls and two boys ranging in age from nine to 18 years of age, essentially maintain the same story over such a long time? If all of the children's stories had been identical, there would have been deserved skepticism and doubt that what was happening there was authentic.

How each of the visionaries developed spiritually and accepted the charismatic role as seers is another crucial part of the success of the apparitions. There were no guidelines to follow; they knew nothing about past apparitions. It was only after Father Jozo gave Mirjana a book on the apparitions at Lourdes that she and the others learned that the Virgin had come before as she was now doing in their village. Mirjana figured that the apparitions in Medjugorje would stop after the Virgin appeared 18 times as she did in Lourdes. All were delighted when they continued past that number.

It would take time for the seers to answer all of the queries and convince the public that what was happening to them was real; believability would increase over time with the consistency of good spiritual fruits. Time, it seems, is always a true measure to claims involving apparitions and other supernatural occurrences.

There has been dramatic change from the youthful visionary of the early days to the mature adult seer of today. Much was made in the beginning of the apparitions that all of them would become priests and nuns. It was taken for granted by the villagers and priests of the parish. As it turned out, *none* of the visionaries would enter religious life, even though Marija and Vicka both professed for more than four years of the active apparitions that they planned to become nuns. Ivan also wanted to become a Franciscan priest. Instead, individually and as a group, they became a strong beacon for family life.

In early August 1981, the visionaries did ask the Virgin if she wanted them to enter religious life. One of them asked, What do you wish that we do later (in life) ? " The Gospa replied, *I would like for you to become priests and religious, but only if you yourselves, would want it. It is up to you to decide.*

Ivanka was the first to decide and her decision was to marry her childhood sweetheart. When the announcement was made, she was chastised by many for not entering a convent. However, she answered in a way that stopped criticism: "Since when is the sacrament of marriage no longer a part of the Church!"

Ivan twice entered a seminary; he would fail both times, unable to handle the academics. Instead, he and all of the visionaries are now married and parents, serving as sterling examples of the sacrament of marriage. Each of them live their life mixed with the responsibility of parenthood and being a visionary. They are seemingly always on call to give personal witness endless times in Medjugorje before massive groups of pilgrims and, by traveling all over the world to do the same. Somehow, all six of the visionaries have managed to live a relatively normal life away from the daunting task given to them by the Blessed Virgin.

As the Madonna continued to appear, the visionaries moved beyond the mere transmission of her messages; they became living examples of them as well. Each assumed a specific task asked by the Madonna. It is essential to know about each of them to comprehend the magnitude of how important the apparitions are as a whole. As noted, Mirjana assumed the role of praying for unbelievers. She was also given special graces, which is why her role was singled out in a separate chapter. However, as stated, it takes nothing away from the other visionaries. Each one of them is crucial to the overall success of the apparitions, which was to change the world and prepare it for what is to come.

Mirjana's good friend **Ivanka** was the first to see the Virgin and was amazed to be included as a visionary. She, too, was typical in her teenage ways. A very attractive dark-haired girl, Ivanka was sure of her path in life. She wanted to marry as quickly as possible and settle in the village to raise her family as part of a lifestyle that had changed little over the centuries.

Like Mirjana, Ivanka has received all ten secrets. She ceased having daily apparitions on May 7, 1985. Ivanka claimed that in the final apparition Our Lady had never looked more sweet and beautiful, and was wearing a beautiful dress, different from the one she normally wore in her apparitions. It sparkled with silver and gold.[1] Her beauty was in contrast to the old home of Ivanka's grandmother, which is where she received her last visit with the Mother of God.

The Virgin was accompanied by two angels—again unusual— with matching outfits. She asked Ivanka if she had a special wish since this was to be her last daily apparition. Yes, Ivanka answered, she wanted to see her deceased mother again (she had experienced this incredible grace several times before). The wish was granted immediately. Ivanka was asked afterward how it felt physically to embrace her mother and also how it felt to touch the Blessed Virgin. She replied, "If I had seen my mom amongst thousands of women,

---

1 The Blessed Mother has appeared in apparition to the Medjugorje visionaries, as well as to the locutionists, in several different dresses. At Christmas, she wears a beautiful white gown trimmed in gold. The locutionists saw her in a very different dress that was white with blue trim.

I would have recognized her. She was the same but much prettier. There was no suffering on her face as she had suffered for years. When she embraced and kissed me, her body was not like our bodies here on earth. I remembered my mom's body; I touched her so many times. But when I touched Our Lady, her body was not like ours, but it was not like my mom's either. She is the Mother of God."

The visionary would later add, "Many people do not believe there is life after this life. But I am here as a living witness, and I can say there is life after life because I was able to see my mom. This witness is not just for me but for all mankind!"

After embraces and kisses, there was a final message given to Ivanka by the Blessed Mother, *My dear child, today is our last meeting. Do not be sad. I shall return on your birthday[2] every year except for this one. My child, do not think that I am not coming because you have done something wrong. You have done nothing wrong. The plans, which my Son and I had, you accepted with your whole heart and you carried them out. Ivanka, the blessings that you and your brothers[3] have received have never previously been accorded to anyone on earth.*

The conversation lasted an hour. Ivanka gave a farewell kiss to Our Lady who then rose aloft to heaven accompanied by the two angels. She now has one apparition a year and states that it is sufficient for her, reiterating what the Virgin had said in her final daily apparition, that she (along with the other seers) has already received more graces than anyone else on earth.

---

2 The Blessed Virgin did not appeare to Ivanka on her birthday, which was June 21, but on June 25, the anniversary of the apparitions. It occurred a year after her last apparition.

3 The reference to "brothers" probably means the other seers, as in the use of the word "mankind".

After experiencing her last daily apparition, Ivanka settled in quietly as just another member of the community. She virtually withdrew from the public as much as possible. She married her childhood sweetheart Rajko Elez on December 29, 1986. They were blessed with three children.

Once her children were grown and on their own, Ivanka resumed giving public witness of her experiences in the village to visiting pilgrims and, on occasion, in other countries. She remains shy and reticent about speaking, far more comfortable simply living the messages as best she can. Her given task is to pray for families. Ironically, that is exactly what she and her family personify.

**Marija** is gifted with an ability to make everyone around her comfortable and at ease. Unobtrusive and humble, she had planned to become a beautician, but after several weeks of the apparitions, she stated she wanted to enter a convent, adding that before the apparitions, God was distant; now, she wanted to give the rest of her life to serving Him.

Plans changed when Marija met a young Italian pilgrim named Paolo Lunetti. They were married in 1993 and now have four children. Marija and her family travel to Medjugorje from their home in Monza, Italy, frequently. They own a home in the village, which also includes a large, separate chapel for her to have her daily apparitions. They have recently added a large retreat center where the visionary has many of her daily apparitions. It is usually filled to standing room only in and around it during the apparition time. This is due to Marija inviting pilgrims to come to her home for the apparition.

Our Lady has asked her as her special purpose to pray for the souls of Purgatory.

I know Marija the best of all the visionaries. I met her in 1986 and was able to tell her my own story of conversion (see the epilogue). I was immediately invited by her to stay at her home whenever I traveled to Medjugorje. Of course, I was overwhelmed. In the succeeding years, I found out how difficult it was to be a visionary. Almost every day, groups of pilgrims would come into the little courtyard of her home begging for her to speak to them. In addition, there always seemed to be three or four other friends staying with her, mostly women—and there was only one small bathroom in the house! There was no heat other than the wood stove in the tiny kitchen. It was a penance and a grace wrapped into one to stay in the home of this extraordinary visionary.

Later, I brought Marija's sister Milka to the United States to learn English. The plan was to send her to school to learn English so that she could become an English-speaking guide for visiting pilgrims. Milka, who saw the Blessed Virgin Mary on the first day of the apparitions (June 24, 1981), but was taken by her mother the next day to a distant field to work, never saw her again in apparition. Like Ivanka, she states that the grace of seeing her just the one time was enough for her. Milka stayed three months with my family and remains a close friend today. However, she did not become a guide but married and is now the mother of three children. The original home of the family is now converted into a place for pilgrims, which is overseen by Milka.

Marija serves an extremely important position by receiving the monthly message from the Blessed Virgin Mary that is meant for the general public. It is given on the 25th day of each month. She has received the monthly messages since March 1987.[4] In her years as a visionary, she has traveled widely to give witness of her experiences, especially in the last three years. She is one of the three visionaries still receiving the daily apparition, along with Ivan and Vicka. It is plausible to speculate that Marija might be the last Medjugorje seer to receive the tenth secret because of her duty of receiving the monthly message. Only she receives it, while the other two active visionaries receive private messages on this day.

I have been present with Marija many times during her apparition, including when she has received the monthly message. I witnessed her receiving and writing it in her own hand. Afterward, she would telephone Medjugorje directly to Father Slavko Barbaric, who would scrutinize it carefully to assure conformance with Holy Scripture and Church doctrine. Only then would it be released for the public. Amazingly, the message makes its way around the world in an extremely short time, usually within an hour.

Once while visiting Marija and Paolo in their apartment home in Monza, Italy, I was with Marija during the daily apparition. Paolo was at work and the usual crowd of Italians normally there each evening somehow did not show up. We were virtually alone, just Marija, her children, and I. During the apparition, I held her youngest child in my lap as the Mother of God appeared to Marija for approximately four minutes. It was the most incredible experience of all such graces, one that assured me personally and professionally of the authenticity of the apparitions. By that, I mean I knew in my heart the reality of what was happening at that precise time. Of course, I

---

4 For three years before receiving the monthly messages, the Virgin would give a weekly message to the villagers, predominantly through Marija.

cannot prove it nor can Marija or any of the visionaries; it is simply a matter of faith in accepting what is felt in the soul.

As we prayed during this particular apparition, waiting for the moment when the Virgin appeared to Marija, two of her children were running around yelling and acting very much as children of their age. When the apparition started, Marija became as a statue, deep in a state of ecstasy. The two little children ran around her, pulling on her and calling out to her. She did not react, remaining focused on the one spot where she saw the Virgin. The only noticeable movement came when the children pulled on her and she swayed slightly. Once the apparition ended, she returned to normal and resumed her duties as mother.

During this visit, I asked Marija if she ever gets tired of being a visionary and all that comes with it. She was in her kitchen cleaning, seemingly haggard and worn out, which is what prompted my question. She turned quickly and began waving a finger at me as she stated with vigor, "Let me tell you, I am a wife, I am a mother and I see Our Lady every day. What more could I possibly want? I have never been so happy!"

In the last three years, Marija has traveled frequently to speak on the apparitions and her role. Her children are now of an age where they can take care of themselves. Paolo's parents live in the same apartment building and are always willing to help with them while Marija travels. Paolo accompanies her when his work allows, but many times, she travels alone.

Like Vicka and Ivan, Marija now has her evening daily apparition often in front of huge crowds. The fact that she and the others have their apparitions in front of crowds, often in Catholic churches, is a positive sign of unofficial approval from the Church. Representatives of the Vatican Commission appointed in 2010 to investigate the authenticity of the Medjugorje apparitions were present at one of Marija's monthly apparitions in the latter part of 2011. They were there to make sure the visionary received the messages in the way she said she does, including writing them down in her own hand. She has been interrogated by the commission several times in the past two years, as well as having a public apparition in a well-known European Catholic Cathedral. Ivan has done the same, once with Marija and twice when just he was present.

**Vicka** easily became the "ambassador" of the apparitions with her cheerful, outgoing personality. She always has a radiant, seemingly perpetual smile on her face. Vicka is the oldest of the seers— and the toughest. That trait led her to share in some of the leadership with Mirjana in the early days of the apparitions. She was given the task to pray for the sick and infirmed, one that brings miraculous healings to many when she prays over them.

Prior to the fateful day when the Blessed Virgin first appeared in the village, Vicka's family had a reputation for having a strong faith. The family could be heard for some distance as they devoutly prayed the prayer of the rosary each evening. The vibrant young girl seemed to have no fear of authority, answering priest and pilgrim alike concerning mundane questions about the apparitions. Once, when a priest made a query about a particular message, and then asked after she had answered, "Are you sure?" Vicka laughed and said, "Of course I'm sure – I was there!"

Another time when local authorities had taken the children to police headquarters for questioning, a police officer threatened Vicka, putting a gun to her temple in an attempt to intimidate her. Testily, she gave a short laugh and said, "Why would you waste a bullet on the likes of me when the economy is so bad?"

It is easy to make the case that Vicka is the most mystical of the visionaries. She "tested the Spirit" of the apparition on the third day by dousing the Blessed Virgin with holy water and stating, "If you are of God, stay, but if not, be gone!" The Virgin simply smiled indicating that she was pleased with the test.

As the apparitions continued, Vicka was asked by the Virgin to take on another task, which was to accept special sufferings. She was requested to do it for "special intentions" as the Mother of God asked her, *Are you willing to accept this?* Vicka did not hesitate in answering in the affirmative.

The first of the visionary's suffering would be a strict fast for several days on nothing but bread and water. Another time, she went into a deep coma for more than 40 days. The suffering continued when the Blessed Virgin Mary asked that Vicka go without seeing her for a specific period of time, ranging up to 40 days. This proved the most difficult and occurred several times. In addition, there would be days when the seer would not receive the daily apparition, while on others she would have multiple visits from the Madonna. In short, the young visionary blessed with so much mysticism literally shared in the redemptive suffering of Jesus by accepting these intentions. It was all for the saving of souls, the Madonna told her.

Vicka stands out as the most mystical of the visionaries because of the special grace of healing prayer she received, one that enables her to pray for the sick and infirmed as asked by the Madonna.

She prays over pilgrims for long stretches of time always seemingly knowing which ones require this special grace. As a result, incredible healings occurred and even more pilgrims flock to Medjugorje in hopes of a similar cure for themselves or a family member.

The ever-smiling seer claims that for two years, from January 7, 1983 until April 10, 1985, Our Lady recounted her life story to her in great detail. It will be published in due course when the Virgin tells her it is time. The other visionaries were also given the story but not in such detail as that given to Vicka.

Vicka received a surprise in early October 1981 while she was at little Jakov's home when the Virgin suddenly appeared and told them that she was going to take them to see heaven. Jakov, frightened and thinking they would not return said, "Why don't you just take Vicka. She has many brothers and sisters, but I am the only child of my mother."

The Virgin smiled and took the two of them by the hand. In a flash, they were in heaven. Vicka wondered how long the journey would take to reach Heaven; she was amazed to find that it took only one second, while the entire trip lasted approximately 20 minutes of earth time. Jakov's mother would report afterward that they completely disappeared from the house for a period of approximately twenty minutes.

Both seers felt a peace they had never experienced before and did not want to leave Heaven. Yet, the journey continued to the edge of hell, where they literally saw a teenage blond girl going into the flames and coming out as a horrendously disfigured animal-like creature. Our Lady apologized for showing them this but said they needed to know that hell does exist and that it is the opposite of Heaven in every way.

Vicka later described Heaven as a wonderfully beautiful place, filled with a sense of peace and happiness that made them want to stay and not return to earthly life. She said that it was filled with people dressed in pastel-colored gowns with no one older than 33 years of age. After showing them this part of paradise and telling them not to be afraid, the Virgin said, *All those who are faithful to God will have that.*

The visionaries described purgatory as a place of gray-brown mist, where they did not actually see anyone but felt anguish and yearning for peace. The seers questioned the Virgin about her reasons for showing them these places, especially paradise. She told them, *I did that so you could see the happiness, which awaits those who love God.* Suddenly, Jesus appeared to them in apparition with injuries covering His body and wearing a crown of thorns. The Blessed Virgin comforted them: *Do not be afraid. It is my Son. See how He has been martyred. In spite of all, He was joyful and He endured all with patience.* The Virgin added: *I am often at Krizevac, at the foot of the cross, to pray there. Now I pray to my Son to forgive the world its sins. The world has begun to convert.*[5]

During this apparition, the Virgin disappeared and the visionaries again saw a terrifying vision of hell. She then reappeared and said: *Do not be afraid! I have shown you hell so that you may know the state of those who are there.* She added: *The devil is trying to conquer us. Do not permit him. Keep the faith, fast, and pray. I will be with you at every step.* The Virgin was indescribable and beautiful light radi-

---

5 The apparition of Jesus is the only known time that the visionaries actually saw Him, other than the first day of the apparitions when the Virgin was holding Him as an infant in her arms. He also appears with her on Christmas day as an infant. Locutionist Jelena would later report that she saw the Lord interiorly one time during her active locutions.

ated, flowed, shined and sparkled around her as she again added, *The people have begun to convert. Keep a solid faith. I need your prayers.*

Vicka stated that this entire experience of seeing Heaven, Purgatory and hell was the most incredible of all her apparitions. The same was true for Jakov.

There is one other important task given to Vicka. The Madonna shared her biography with the visionaries, giving each details of her life; Vicka received more than the others in far greater detail and length. Our Lady told her to remember it well and to write it down because the time would come when she would be given permission to share it with the world. Vicka has three notebooks of dictations. According to one source, a priest has been chosen who will see to its publication. The notebooks are written in a special script that Vicka stated, "When the time comes for us to see and understand that, we will be able to do that."

In January 2002, the enigmatic Vicka, the one visionary everyone was sure would become a nun, shocked the followers of the apparitions by marrying a long-time friend, Mario Mijatovic. She was the oldest of the visionaries and the last to marry. They live in the parish of Medjugorje and have two children, making her role more difficult, especially since the sufferings continue. Yet, as Vicka related to me in an informal interview, they manage and she happily accepts whatever is asked of her by God.

As a teenager, **Ivan** was almost the direct opposite of Vicka. Extremely shy and introverted, he was visibly uncomfortable around pilgrims and the media and did not enjoy the notoriety of being a visionary. The seer was in a constant state of awe that the Virgin had chosen him. He later explained that when he first saw the image of the Virgin on the hillside, he ran away out of fear that he had never really acknowledged God as a part of his life. Ivan immediately went to his room, locked the door and began to pray. His mother was stunned, and would later state that she believed her son was actually seeing the Blessed Virgin when she found a rosary in his jean pocket as she was doing the laundry.

Ivan would enter a seminary in August, just two months after the apparitions began. He was sure this was his calling and wanted to please the Madonna who had asked all of the visionaries to consider a religious vocation. He failed and then tried again in 1982. Both attempts ended with his inability to handle the academic requirements. Yet, the desire and effort indicated just how deeply he was spiritually moved with the realization that the Blessed Mother was appearing daily to him and the others at Medjugorje. As time would eventually confirm, the Virgin had other plans for him. He would overcome all shyness to become a very accomplished witness to the graces of Medjugorje.

Given his shyness, it is near miraculous that the young Ivan began traveling the world to give witness to Medjugorje after his failure to be a priest. Somehow, he was able to overcome an introversion that was so severe, that he would cross a road to prevent having to speak to a stranger in his village. As more pilgrims came to Medjugorje and showed up at his house to hear his witness, he slowly was able to overcome his fear of being with strangers. Today, Ivan is in high demand as a speaker, especially in the United States. He was the first visionary to have his daily apparitions in public before large crowds in churches and conferences.

In October 1994, Ivan married an American woman from Boston, Laureen Murphy, who is a former Miss Massachusetts. They met during one of his frequent visits to the states. They have three children. The family divides time between modest homes in Medjugorje and Boston.

Recently in a talk on June 24, 2011 during the anniversary of the apparition's celebration in the village, Ivan gave some interesting comments: "Many people ask me if Our Lady has ever talked about the second coming of Jesus," he said. "The answer is no. Has Our Lady talked about the end of the world? Again, no. Our Lady hasn't come because of that. So many ask, what does Our Lady say? What do you talk about, with her every day? We talk a lot. Believe me, if we had 24 hours, we would miss some (only a few) minutes. But one day when the time comes, when some things get revealed, you will understand why the apparitions are such a long time and why every day... Later on, our eyes will be opened... When we see physical changes that are going to happen in the world... This is so important to understand... The time in front of us is the time of great responsibility."

The shy young Ivan has come a long way.

The question on the minds of many villagers was what was nine-year-old **Jakov** doing among the selected visionaries? A clever, impish, strong-headed boy, so like other young boys his age, Jakov was hardly what one would expect to play an integral part in such a miracle. His interests were far from prayer and church attendance; closer to the mark was an interest in sports, especially soccer. Even after his inclusion as a visionary, he was not above once asking the Madonna to tell him the score of an upcoming championship soccer match, which included one of his favorite teams! The Virgin merely smiled.

Jakov's father was rarely present in their small hovel of a home. He was constantly away working as a migrant worker in Austria, leaving the task of raising and providing for his only son to his wife. When Jakov was eight years old, his father abandoned the family. He was left an orphan at the age of 12 when his mother died in 1983. After her death, he moved into the home of his uncle.

The little boy immersed himself in games as an escape from the harsh realities of daily life. Once the visions became a regular part of each day, Jakov was always in attendance at the evening Mass. He spoke with awe about the Virgin. Her daily appearance became the most important part of his life, and he spoke with seriousness and pointed politeness when interviewed by media and priests.

Vicka spent more time with little Jakov than the other visionaries. She believed there was something special about the boy in his relationship with Gospa, even though it was a mystery to her. When asked by her confessor why Our Lady chose little Jakov, Vicka said, "I can't say that I know that. None of you really know the little guy! I always remember how the Virgin at the very start said: 'The rest of you go, and let little Jakov remain with me'. That is an unusual boy."

Any 10-year-old would consider it impossible to endure up to three hours of prayer and attendance at church. How could someone so young be on their knees every single night, year after year, without any break in the routine? If the apparitions had been a trick or a lie conceived by the so-called visionaries, little Jakov would have broken a long time ago—and yet, it is said of him that he was the most faithful in attendance to the evening prayer services among the visionaries.

Life became more than bearable after the apparitions started. Jakov married at age of 22 a beautiful Italian girl, Annalisa Barozzi. Today they have three children and reside in Medjugorje.

Jakov's daily apparitions went on for more than 17 years—until September 12, 1998. The Virgin confided the tenth and last secret to him during an apparition while he and his family, along with Mirjana, were in Miami, Florida for a series of talks. As with Mirjana and Ivanka before him, Jakov had a hard time coping with the fact his daily encounters with the Virgin were over. It was understandable since he had spent a majority of his life seeing her every day. Mirjana did everything possible to console the young man.

With a gentle smile, the Blessed Mother said to her youngest seer, *Dear child, I am your mother and I love you unconditionally. From today, I will not be appearing to you every day, but only on Christmas, the birthday of my Son. Do not be sad, because as a mother, I will always be with you and like every true mother, I will never leave you. And you continue further to follow the way of my Son, the way of peace and love, and try to persevere in the mission that I have confided to you. Be an example of that man who has known God and God's love. Let people always see in you an example of how God acts on people and how God acts through them. I bless you with my motherly blessing and I thank you for having responded to my call.*

The Blessed Virgin's words were comforting to him; still, Jakov cried and was inconsolable for a long time. He had cried most of the previous day when the Blessed Virgin had first told him that the next day would be his final, daily apparition. The normally jocular

Jakov was subdued as he traveled in the Southern Florida region giving talks.

Several days later, Jakov went to the poverty-stricken nation of Haiti, where more than 70,000 people came to hear the message of Medjugorje. A quieter, mature Jakov was beginning a new phase of service as a witness of how God acts on people – and through them.

Something special happened to Jakov on the feast of Our Lady's Nativity, September 8, 1981. The Virgin appeared to Vicka and Jakov in his house. The little boy held out his hand to the Virgin, saying: "Dear Holy Virgin, I wish you a happy birthday." Gospa then shook his hand. He was in awe.

The picture of Jakov's face, eager and upturned in the early years of the apparitions, is one of the most external signs that give proof of the apparitions. Possibly, that look of innocence is the reason why he was included as a visionary.

Through the abridged bios of the visionaries, one can see the variety of personalities the Virgin chose to be conveyers of her Heavenly messages. Yet, each was chosen for a specific reason in order to bring success to her last apparitions. Some were given more responsibility than the others. Each has lived up to her desires according to her early and recent messages.

Above all gifts given to the visionaries, the remarkable and miraculous grace of healing prayer stands out. Vicka has been the major instrument of this Holy Spirit gift at Medjugorje. Through her healing prayers have come a myriad of graces for thousands. Of all of those, one healing stands out above the rest. It is the healing of a woman who had 16 major illnesses when she came to Medjugorje. She left with none.

*Dear children, I am with you and I am not giving up. I desire to have you come to know my Son. I desire for my children to be with me in eternal life. I desire for you to feel the joy of peace and to have eternal salvation. I am praying that you may overcome human weaknesses. I am imploring my Son to give you pure hearts. My dear children, only pure hearts know how to carry a cross and know how to sacrifice for all those sinners who have offended the Heavenly Father and who, even today, offend Him, although they have not come to know Him. I am praying that you may come to know the light of true faith, which comes only from prayer of pure hearts. It is then that all those who are near you will feel the love of my Son. Pray for those whom my Son has chosen to lead you on the way to salvation. May your mouth refrain from every judgment. Thank you.*

—Given to Mirjana on August 2, 2012.

> And when they bring you before the synagogues and the rulers and the authorities, do not be anxious how or what you are to answer or what you are to say: for the Holy Spirit will teach you in that very hour what you ought to say.
>
> —Luke 12: 11-12.

## CHAPTER XII:

## JELENA AND MARIANA: A NEW DIMENSION

AS IF APPEARING to the six visionaries was not enough grace, the Blessed Virgin Mary added a new dimension to the apparitions as they continued daily into 1983. A ten-year-old girl from the village suddenly began conversations with the Blessed Virgin in a fashion different from the visionaries. She could "hear" and "see" her but in a very different way.

While in class at school, little Jelena Vasilj began hearing a gentle voice speaking to her interiorly. The words were of routine things at first, as though allowing the child to familiarize herself with the process. A few days later, Jelena discovered the "source" of the inner voice. She told her family and the priests of the village, "I saw and heard the angel who prepared me for the coming of Our Lady . . . He didn't say so, but I knew he was my guardian angel."

Thus, after her guardian angel "prepared" Jelena, the Blessed Virgin came to her on December 29. She spoke to the little girl but did not appear interiorly at first. When she did, it was in a different way than that of the six visionaries. Jelena described it as inner words and inner visions. She saw "with the heart" whereas the six visionaries see Mary in a vivid three-dimensional way, just as one normally sees someone else. They see her with their eyes shut or open. Jelena's locutions occurred two or three times in a day rather than one apparition in the evening to the visionaries. She would prepare herself as they did with a period of prayer.

Three months later, another ten-year-old, and close friend of Jelena, who was frequently in prayer with her before her locutions, began experiencing the same grace. Marijana Vasilj (not related) became the eighth youth in the village to experience the presence of Gospa. She would later describe to a priest how the young locutionists saw her. Marijana said, "First, a white cloud comes that disappears when Our Lady comes. She is all in white and wears a crown of stars held together by themselves 'without a wire,' and a rosary hangs from her folded hands."

Marijana also stated that Jesus sometimes accompanied the Virgin during the interior visions, something that only happened once with the visionaries. She described Jesus as being seen only from the waist up, having long black hair and wearing a gray robe with a red cape.[1] She added that He was only seen and that He never spoke during these sessions, although He sometimes smiled.

In May 1983, the Virgin began giving Jelena teachings concerning the spiritual life. She told her to write the teachings down because she was to entrust them later to Church authorities. By this time, Jelena could speak to the Virgin at will but only on spiritual matters. The Blessed Virgin told her that all she needed to know is

---

1 This description of Jesus by the locutionist is slightly different from that given by the visionaries where he is described as having "brown" hair.

written in the Gospels, that she should read and believe it, and that she would find all the answers there.

While the mission of these two young people receiving locutions is complementary to that of the six visionaries, they were informed by Mary that it would be different later. They would not receive the ten secrets that were given to the others, but they seemed to receive stronger, more detailed messages of spirituality, most especially Jelena. Still, their responsibility was not quite on the same spiritual plane as the visionaries.

After four months of preparing her two new children, the Blessed Virgin asked Jelena to advise her spiritual director that she would like a prayer group in the parish comprised of young people. Guidelines given by Gospa asked members to voluntarily commit to four years of total consecration to God, putting aside all decisions concerning the future during this time. They were asked to meet three times a week, to pray at least three hours daily, go to Mass frequently, and fast on bread and water twice a week. These guidelines would become the standard for similar prayer groups throughout the world, inspired by the apparitions at Medjugorje.

The first meeting of the prayer group took place in the basement of the rectory on a Tuesday evening. Interestingly, the Virgin's first message to the group was to love their enemies: *I know that you are not able to love your enemies, but I beg you to pray every day at least five minutes to the Sacred Heart, and to my Heart, and we will give you the divine love with which you will be able to love even your enemies.*

It is believed that the Virgin was again referring to her plea for peace and reconciliation between the three cultures that made up the population of the area. Without peace among the three groups, it would be difficult to develop the network to spread her messages in the region and then throughout the world.

As had been the case in the first year and a half of apparitions, the Blessed Virgin again emphasized to the locutionists and the members of the prayer group that prayer was the true pathway to learning spiritual love. She pointedly reminded the people of the ethnic divisions within the region. Such a message was especially important to the young who are potentially more capable of changing traditional hatreds than adults who have had them ingrained from decades of conflict.

The young people's prayer group grew in spiritual intensity and in numbers. Two months later, the Madonna told the group: *You have decided to follow Jesus, to consecrate yourselves totally to Him. Now, when a person decides to follow God totally, Satan comes along and tries to remove that person from the path on which they have set out. This is the time of testing. He will try by all means to lead you astray. Satan will tell you: 'This is too much. This is nonsense. You can be Christians like everybody else. Don't pray, don't fast.' I tell you, this is the time when you must persevere in your fast and your prayers. You must not listen to Satan. Do what I have told you. Satan can do nothing to those who believe in God and have totally abandoned themselves to him. But you are inexperienced and so I urge you to be careful.*

Over time, it became evident that Jelena would be given the majority of the messages from the Blessed Virgin. Marijana slowly stopped receiving the locutions but continued to participate in the prayer group. It appears that the messages given to Jelena will play a very important part when the apparitions cease to all the visionaries and locutionists. They could conceivably be a vital part of preparation before the start of the secrets.

Here is a sampling of messages and teachings Jelena received on a daily basis from the locutions:

### Wednesday, December 29, 1982

Jelena asks Gospa: May I know the ten secrets? Mary's answer: *I did not appear to you as to the other six because my plan is different. To them I entrusted messages and secrets. Forgive me if I cannot tell you the secrets which I have entrusted to them; it concerns a grace which is for them, but not for you. I appeared to you for the purpose of helping you to progress in spiritual life and through your intermediary I want to lead people to holiness.*

### Beginning of 1983

Jelena asks the Blessed Virgin about the authenticity of the apparitions of the six visionaries, and on the sign, which has been promised: Our Lady's answer: *Pardon me, but you cannot know it; it is a special gift for them. You will have to believe it like all the others. In the meantime, everything that they say corresponds to truth.*

### Tuesday, March 1, 1983

To Jelena: *Transcribe all the lessons which I give you for the spiritual life; later you will deliver them to the authorities of the Church.*[2]

---

2 The Virgin gives confirmation that her teachings to Jelena and Mirijana are for the Church after the apparitions to the six visionaries end.

**April 4, 1983** (Easter Monday)

Mary tells Jelena: *Do not pity anyone. If the police cause you some anxiety, continue on your way joyful and calm. Pray for them. When God begins His work, no one can stop it.*

**December 15, 1982.**

The Virgin gives a message to Jelena: *Hurry to be converted. Do not wait for the great sign. For the unbelievers, it will then be too late to be converted. For you who have the faith, this time constitutes a great opportunity for you to be converted, and to deepen your faith. Fast on bread and water before every feast, and prepare yourselves through prayer. Fast once a week on bread and water in honor of the Holy Spirit outside of Friday. Have the largest possible number of persons pray and fast during the novena of the Holy Spirit, so that it may spread over the church. Fast and pray for the Bishop.*

**Wednesday, April 20, 1983**

To Jelena, the Blessed Virgin is in tears: *I give all the graces to those who commit grave sins, but they do not convert. Pray! Pray for them! Do not wait for Friday. Pray now. Today your prayers and your penance are necessary to me.*

As is evident, the messages to Jelena and Marijana are similar to those given to the visionaries. In due time her teachings became focused on special teachings and two specific consecrations to be prayed by the prayer group. Here are the astonishing consecrations that the Blessed Mother gave to Jelena:

**Consecration to the Heart of Jesus** (Given to Jelena on November 28,1983)

*O Jesus, we know that You are sweet (Mt. 11:29). That you have given Your heart for us.*
*It was crowned with thorns by our sins.*
*We know that today, You still pray for us so that we will not be lost.*
*Jesus, remember us if we fall into sin.*
*Through Your most Sacred Heart, make us all love one another.*
*Cause hatred to disappear among men. Show us Your love. All of us love You.*
*And we desire that you protect us with Your Heart of the Good Shepherd.*
*Enter into each heart, Jesus! Knock on the door of our hearts.*
*Be patient and tenacious with us. We are still locked up in ourselves, because we have not understood Your will.*
*Knock continuously, Oh Jesus. Make our hearts open up to you, at least in reminding us of the passion which you suffered for us.*
*Amen*

**Consecration to the Immaculate Heart of Mary** (Given on November 28,1983)

*O Immaculate Heart of Mary, overflowing with goodness,*
*Show us your love for us.*
*May the flame of your heart, Oh Mary, Descend upon all peoples.*
*We love you immensely.*
*Impress in our hearts a true love.*
*May our hearts yearn for you.*

*Oh Mary, sweet and humble of heart, remember us when we sin.*
*You know that all mankind are sinners.*
*Through your most sacred and maternal heart, cure us from every*
*spiritual illness.*
*Make us capable of looking at the beauty of your maternal heart,*
*And that, thus, we may be converted to the flame of your heart.*
*Amen*

There is no need to go further into the incredible graces given to the two young inner locutionists, Jelena and Marijana. They are often overlooked or forgotten by the followers of the Medjugorje apparitions. Yet, as can be seen by the power of the consecrations given to Jelena, they are an integral part of the grace of Medjugorje.

Marijana would eventually marry and settle in the village. Her locutions ceased and she settled into life as wife and mother.

Jelena, who is extremely brilliant, would progress in education to attending school in Rome and earning a doctorate degree in theology. She married an Italian man named Massimiliano Valente in August 2002. Her locutions would eventually fade away, leaving her as desolate as the visionaries when they received the last of the ten secrets. She is a mother of three beautiful children today and lives in Italy with her family.

Needless to say, the most important good fruits of Medjugorje are the tremendous spiritual conversions that have occurred. Physical healings, though, are the most dramatic. No healing that has occurred at Medjugorje is more dramatic or sensational than the healing of a woman from America, who came to the village with numerous major illnesses and conditions.

*Dear children! Also today I call you to prayer. Little children, believe that by simple prayer miracles can be worked. Through your prayer you open your heart to God and He works miracles in your life. By looking at the fruits, your heart fills with joy and gratitude to God for everything He does in your life and, through you, also to others. Pray and believe little children, God gives you graces and you do not see them. Pray and you will see them. May your day be filled with prayer and thanksgiving for everything that God gives you. Thank you for having responded to my call.*

—Message given to Marija on October 25, 2002.

> And Jesus answered them, "Go and tell John what you hear and see: the blind receive their sight and the lame walk, lepers are cleansed and the deaf hear, and the dead are raised up, and the poor have good news preached to them.
>
> —Matthew 11: 4-5.

## CHAPTER XIII: COLLEEN'S MIRACULOUS HEALING

MIRACULOUS HEALINGS have occurred at Medjugorje from the beginning days of the apparitions. Relatives brought the sick and handicapped, begging the visionaries to ask Gospa's intercession for a healing. Many stupendous healings have occurred in Medjugorje. They continue to happen and in all likelihood it will occur right up to the last apparition.

The first healing took place during the first days of the apparitions when the parents of a handicapped child desperately begged the visionaries to ask Gospa to intercede on his behalf. The little boy, whose name is Daniel, could neither hear nor speak and he walked with a limp. The visionaries were touched and they complied, putting the question to the Virgin. She answered after looking at little Daniel and his family for a long time: *Have them believe strongly in his cure. Go in the peace of God.*

Implausibly, the parents were disappointed in the answer, a very human response in retrospect. They had expected immediate healing for their child. The Virgin Mary was telling them to pray, to have faith and to trust.

Fortunately for the little boy, the parents obeyed even if somewhat reluctantly. They wondered why Gospa did not intercede on behalf of their son immediately. Still, they listened and prayed fervently and continuously as they began the long trip to their home. Later that evening, the family stopped at a small restaurant for dinner. The day's event at Medjugorje dominated the conversation. Suddenly, little Daniel grabbed a cup and banged it on the table, exclaiming in a loud voice, "Momma, I want milk!" they were all astounded and fully aware now of what the Virgin meant when she called for prayer and belief. Several months later, Daniel could hear and speak; soon, he was running and playing with other boys. Daniel is now in his late thirties and completely healthy.

Since the healing of Daniel, many more have occurred. Each little miracle continues to supply proof of the success of the apparitions along with the other factors discussed in earlier chapters. However, one particular healing stands out as arguably the most stunning. It is the healing of Colleen Willard from Chicago, Illinois. It took place in September 2003.

Colleen Willard came to Medjugorje unable to walk without canes and a wheelchair. She was so weakened from her infirmities that she could barely talk and hold her head upright.

Besides having an inoperable brain tumor, which alone threatened to end her life, there were at least 15 other *major* ailments. There was something called Hashimoto's thyroiditis, myofascial fibromyalgia, severe osteomalacia, critical adrenal insufficiency—and so many complications from all of them that no airline wanted to accept the responsibility of her flying the long journey to Medjugorje.

Even Medjugorje tour leaders Jack and Gail Boos, who had been taking pilgrims to Medjugorje for numerous years, were hesitant to accept her because of the complicated medical conditions. A physician's clearance was required. Somehow, a doctor eventually signed off on the trip and medical clearance came through, an act nearly as miraculous as the healing itself. Once medical clearance was obtained, Jack and Gail reluctantly agreed to take Colleen and husband John on their pilgrimage to the village.

Colleen accompanied the group to Vicka's house in the early morning the day after arriving in Medjugorje. Vicka was speaking that morning and the group wanted to get there early enough to allow Colleen to be positioned near the front. She was placed in her wheelchair by the owner of the home that was hosting the group and then driven to Vicka's original house where she usually gave her talks.

After driving Colleen and husband John to the site, their host then pushed Colleen through the tightly packed crowd, trying to get her close to the visionary. However, all of the people around her were pushing her and leaning on her while jostling for a better position to see the visionary. Mothers were bringing their children in and passing them over her head, constantly bumping and touching her. At one point, Gail feared for Colleen's life. "I made a horrible mistake by bringing her up here," she thought. "Please Lord, forgive me. This is too much for her!"

Suddenly, Colleen's head dropped and Gail was sure she had died. Colleen had told Gail before coming on the pilgrimage that she could die at any moment if the pituitary gland gave way or her head was banged too hard. One of her conditions was so severe that she could barely tolerate being touched as it resulted in searing pain.

Now the crowd bumped and pushed her to the side. Her husband John was far back in the crowd. Seeing what was happening, he frantically pushed his way through to her side, lifted her head back, put some morphine mixed with another medicine under her tongue—and prayed. It took Colleen quite some time to revive.

Vicka saw what was happening as she was speaking. As soon as she finished, she pushed her way through the crowd, ignoring those grabbing at her. She approached Colleen and kept repeating in English "Praise God! Praise God!"

The visionary then opened her arms, reached inside Colleen's wheelchair and pulled her into her chest hugging and kissing her. Then she put her left hand on Colleen's head. As she went to place her right hand on her as well, pilgrims literally pulled her hand away from Colleen and stuffed prayer petitions, rosaries and pictures into it. Yet, Vicka, with her beautiful heavenly presence and smile, continued fervently praying over Colleen.

The raucous crowd suddenly became hushed, knowing something special was happening. Colleen would later state that as Vicka was praying over her, she felt a strong heat throughout her body. Many could see what looked like a golden globe coming from Vicka's hand. Colleen would say later that day, "My head felt like coals! My head was burning! It was like a hot spiral going through my body!"

When Vicka finished praying over the limp body of Colleen a seemingly long time, but about 10 minutes, she bent over, hugged and kissed her again. Amazingly, there was no pain from Vicka's hugging and touching her. Minutes later, the villager who had brought her to the talk now got Colleen into a taxi so they could get to the church in time for the morning Mass.

Once inside the packed church, John rolled Colleen to the very front. Jack and Gail stayed at the back, happy that Vicka had prayed over Colleen and now were praying for a miracle. It was about to occur.

As Colleen sat in her wheelchair, she could still feel the heat from Vicka's hands on her. Later, she shared that when the priest began to consecrate the host, she heard the Blessed Mother say, *My daughter, will you surrender to God the Father? Will you surrender to my Spouse, the Holy Spirit? Will you surrender to my Son, Jesus?* Colleen then heard the Blessed Mother add, *Will you surrender now?*

In a state beyond the presence of the real world, Colleen answered with humility and joy, "Yes, I will surrender now, all for the glory of heaven, all for the glory of God".

At that moment, Colleen began to feel her legs tingle.

Colleen reported that when she heard the Blessed Virgin Mary speaking so tenderly and lovingly to her, "It went through my entire being." She added, "When she spoke to my heart I couldn't hear any other words that were being said. When the Eucharist was placed on my tongue, immediately at that point I was aware of heat leaving; and, when the heat was leaving, the pain that I had endured for years, 24 hours a day, suddenly started to go away. After Holy Communion, John looked at me but said nothing. He saw on my face what was happening and got down on his knees next to the wheelchair. I smiled at him and said calmly, "John, please get me out of this wheelchair. It feels cumbersome. I can move my hands, I can move my arms; look, there's no pain!"

To the shock of John and the others, Colleen was able to get out of the chair and stand. There was no sign of any infirmities and she seemed suddenly strong and able.

When the group returned to their lodging place, they discovered what had happened to their fellow pilgrim. Some had seen Vicka praying over Colleen but no one was fully aware of what happened in the church during Mass. Now, they saw her standing, laughing and moving about freely. Everyone was in tears of joy. At one point, Colleen asked John to dance with her and as they did, the group applauded and shouted praises to God.

During the celebration, the owner of the house returned and walked in as John and Colleen were dancing. Bewildered, he began to speak rapidly in Croatian; it was evident that he was confused—and angry. He thought that Colleen was not really ill, that he had been duped into believing it. It took some time for his wife and others to convince him that Colleen had been healed and that it was a miracle. Soon, he joined in the celebration.

Shortly after returning home from the pilgrimage, Colleen went to her doctor in Chicago, a pulmonary specialist. She walked up to the reception desk and said, "I'm Colleen Willard", a redundancy since everyone in the office knew her by sight. "No, you're not," they kept saying, shaking their heads in disbelief of what they were seeing. Colleen held out her arms and said, "Oh, yes, I am!"

Pandemonium swept the medical office. Employees were screaming and running through the office yelling for Colleen's doctor, "Dr. Duggan, Dr. Duggan, come here!" Baffled by the excitement in his office he quickly walked into the reception area and saw his patient Colleen standing there smiling. All he could say was, "Oh my God! Oh my God! Oh my God!"

Just as life had radically changed with the discovery of Colleen Willard's brain tumor, other major illnesses and conditions, life changed again. In place of months of appointments with doctors and health institutions trying to find some kind of medical relief for the beleaguered wife and mother, Colleen was now on a near constant speaking schedule to tell her story. The slumped over figure who seemed at times to be in a semi-comatose state due to the chronic suffering from the illnesses, was replaced by a vibrant woman filled with energy.

The story of the healing of Colleen serves as major proof of what God can do when a soul is open to His grace. It is also awesome evidence of the spiritual authenticity of the Medjugorje apparitions.


The Mother of Jesus is not the iconic figure seen in early medieval paintings and statues. She is a human being given the great grace to be the mother of Jesus. What has been discovered through the apparitions in the village is that she is *very* human, *very* personal even though she is a heavenly figure. Mary is intimate, loving and warm in her conversations with the visionaries. She is also very much the teacher as can be seen in the early-day exchanges with the visionaries.

Hear her words now. Though they were spoken to her chosen seers, they are meant as teachings and guidance for all of her children.

*Through fasting and prayer, one can stop wars; one can suspend the laws of nature...*

—To the visionaries as part of a message on fasting; given on April 21, 1982.

> After this, many of his disciples drew back and no longer went about with him. Jesus said to the twelve, "Will you also go away? "Simon Peter answered him, "Lord to whom shall we go? You have the words of eternal life."
>
> —John 6: 66-68.

## CHAPTER XIV: HER WORDS TO THE WORLD

IMAGINE THE improbable grace of knowing the actual words spoken to the visionaries in the early years of the apparitions. That grace becomes reality as we share in the intimacy and informality of the conversations between the Blessed Virgin Mary and her seers.

The messages given to the visionaries as a group and individually by the Blessed Virgin during the first two years of the apparitions are informal and revealing, sometimes even shocking. Usually she gave them on a daily basis; on rare occasions, she skipped a day. Occasionally, she would appear multiple times giving additional messages and teachings. It was a period of learning and becoming familiar with the woman from Heaven.

The selection of the period from June 1981 to June 1983 provides an intimate glimpse at how the Blessed Virgin Mary developed a relationship with her visionaries as she instructed them and generally confirmed segments of Catholic Church doctrine as well as parts of Holy Scripture. The earliest messages were carefully recorded by the parish in Medjugorje. Unfortunately, they were confiscated and destroyed by the communists in August 1981, when they came to arrest Father Jozo Zovko.

Fortunately, nearly all of the destroyed messages were meticulously gleaned from the works of internationally acclaimed leading Marian theologian Father René Laurentin, and Professor René LeJeune, two of the most noted theologians in France. They received them directly from painstaking interviews with the visionaries. Great care was taken in their recording, translation, and compilation. Virtually all of them were confirmed by the seers over time.

The number of messages in this period have been edited to focus on those that address the most relevant issues. Personal comments from the seers are included to give a complete picture of just how intimate the Virgin is with her children. I have also inserted short commentaries on selected messages for clarification. The commentaries will be in non-bold italics, while the words of the Virgin are in bold italics.

We begin with the first words spoken by the Blessed Virgin Mary to her new visionaries on June 25, 1981: ***Praise be to Jesus!***

Ivanka asks, "Where is my mother?" (Her mother had died two months previously.) The Virgin responds with a smile, ***She is happy. She is with me.***

Mirjana: No one will believe us. They will say that we are crazy. Give us a sign! The apparition responds only with a smile. Mirjana later believed she had received a sign because her watch had changed time during the apparition.

Ivanka: Why have you come here? What do you desire? ***I have come because there are many true believers here. I wish to be with you to convert and to reconcile the whole world.***

**Monday, June 29, 1981**

The visionaries: Dear Gospa, are you happy to see so many people here today? *More than happy. (She smiles).* How long will you stay with us? *As long as you will want me to, my angels.* What do you expect of the people who have come in spite of the brambles and the heat? *There is only one God, one faith. Let the people believe firmly and do not fear anything.* What do you expect of us? *That you have a solid faith and that you maintain confidence.* Will we know how to endure persecutions, which will come to us because of you? *You will be able to, my angels. Do not fear. You will be able to endure everything. You must believe and have confidence in me.*

*Commentary: during the period June 30 to December 31, the Virgin appeared to the visionaries in hidden places, away from the police patrols that were trying to track them down. That is why the latter was asked.*

Mirjana then asked, "Would you be angry if we would not return any longer to the hill, but we would wait in the church? After hesitating momentarily, she replied *Always at the same time. Go in the peace of God.*

**Thursday, July 2, 1981**

Jakov: Dear Gospa, leave us a sign. The Virgin seemed to consent with a nod: *Goodbye, my dear angels.*

*Commentary: Here is the first reference to a sign that the young seers wanted to prove they are actually seeing her. Eventually, it would be revealed to be the third secret or warning to the world that the apparitions were from God.*

One of the visionaries ask where is Paradise and the Kingdom of God? Mary answers, *In Heaven.*

Our Lady is asked if she is the Mother of God and if she went to heaven before or after her death. She responds, *I am the Mother of God and the Queen of Peace. I went to Heaven before death.*[1]

Again they ask, when will the sign be left? *I will not yet leave the sign. I shall continue to appear. Father Jozo sends you greetings. He is experiencing difficulties, but he will resist, because he knows why he is suffering.*

### October 17, 1981

Once more about the sign: *It is mine to realize the promise. With respect to the faithful, have them pray and believe firmly.*

### October 19, 1981

The Virgin tells the children: *Pray for Father Jozo and fast tomorrow on bread and water. Then you will fast for a whole week on bread and water. Pray, my angels. Now I will show you Father Jozo.* She shows them a vision of Father Jozo in prison and tells them not to fear for him because everything will work out fine.

### October 21, 1981

Because Vicka is concerned about Fr. Jozo's sentencing and knows that Our Lady is not motivated by vengeance, she begs her to intercede that the people involved be reasonable and impartial. *Jozo looks well and he greets you warmly. Do not fear for Jozo. He is a saint. I have already told you. Sentence will not be pronounced this evening. Do not be afraid, he will not be condemned to a severe punishment.*

---

1 This statement by the Blessed Virgin gives unofficial authentication to the Catholic Church doctrine of the Assumption of the Blessed Virgin Mary.

*Pray only, because Jozo asks from you prayer and perseverance. Do not be afraid because I am with you.*

## October 22, 1981

The Virgin tells the visionaries, *Jozo has been sentenced. Let us go to church to pray.* The visionaries tell Our Lady they are saddened because of Father Jozo. She responds, *You should rejoice!* The visionaries ask if the whiteness of the cross is a supernatural phenomenon, as it was seen by many of the villagers earlier. *Yes, I confirm it.* Many saw the cross transform itself into a light and then into a silhouette of Our Lady. She tells them, *All of these signs are designed to strengthen your faith until I leave you the visible and permanent sign.*

In a rare admonishment, the Virgin tells Ivanka in a firm but gentle way: *Pray more. The others are praying and suffering more than you.*

The Madonna tells the visionaries: *Tell the young people not to allow themselves to be distracted from the true way. Let them remain faithful to their religion.*

## October, 1981

The Blessed Mother comments on the state of several countries once under the oppression of Communism. Regarding Poland: *There will be great conflicts, but in the end, the just will take over.* she then confirms what she stated during her appearances in Fatima regarding Russia: *The Russian people will be the people who will glorify God the most. The West has made civilization progress, but without God, as if they were their own creators.*

*Commentary: this is a critical message for the west, which, of course, includes America. She would later state that confession is the solution for the west to return to God.*

## November 6, 1981

During this apparition, Our Lady disappears and the visionaries see a terrifying vision of Hell. Then she reappears and says to them: *Do not be afraid! I have shown you Hell so that you may know the state of those who are there.*

## December 8, 1981

Gospa answers questions the visionaries have about their futures. *I would like all of you to become priests and religious, but only if you desire it. You are free. It is up to you to choose. If you are experiencing difficulties or if you need something, come to me. If you do not have the strength to fast on bread and water, you can give up a number of things. It would be a good thing to give up television, because after seeing some programs, you are distracted and unable to pray. You can give up alcohol, cigarettes, and other pleasures. You yourselves know what you have to do.* Our Lady then kneels down profoundly serious, with her hands extended. She prays to Jesus: *My beloved Son, I beseech you to be willing to forgive the world its great sin through which it offends you.*

## December 9, 1981

While we (visionaries) were praying, the Madonna intervened: *Oh my Son Jesus, forgive these sins; there are so many of them!* We stopped and became silent and Gospa added, *Continue to pray, because prayer is the salvation of the people.*

## December 25, 1981 Christmas

The visionaries see Baby Jesus. The Blessed Virgin says to them, *Love one another, my children. You are brothers and sisters. Don't argue among yourselves. Give glory to God, glorify Him and sing, my angels.*

## March 4, 1982

The visionaries ask a questions regarding a woman who had no children: *Let her believe firmly. God, who comes to help everyone, will likewise help her. Be patient, my angels, do not be afraid of anything. I am at your side and guard you. If you have any problems, whatever it be, call me. I will come immediately and help you in advising you on best resolving the difficulty. Go in peace, my angels. Good-bye.*

## April 11, 1982 (Easter Sunday)

The Virgin comments concerning the formation of prayer groups: *It is necessary, but not only here. Communities of prayer are necessary in all parishes.*

## May 2, 1982

The Virgin makes a powerful statement concerning the purpose of her apparitions in Medjugorje: *"I have come to call the world to conversion for the last time. Afterwards, I will not appear any more on this earth."*

*Commentary: This message confirms the major premise of this book in that the Virgin Mary states she will never come to earth in apparition again. It is one of the most meaningful messages given at Medjugorje.*

## June 24, 1982

The Blessed Mother tells the seers, *Thank the people in my name for the prayers, the sacrifices, and the* (acts of) *penance. Have them persevere in prayer, fasting, and conversion and have them wait with patience for the realization of my promise. Everything is unfolding according to God's plan.*

## July 12, 1982

Gospa gives the visionaries another critical message when asked if there will be another world war. She answers: *The third world war will not take place.*

*Commentary: She reassures there will not be a third world war. However, she predicts that there will be many small or regional conflicts, many of which will be more devastating.*

## July 21, 1982

She answers a question concerning Purgatory: *There are many souls in Purgatory. There are also persons who have been consecrated to God - some priests, some religious. Pray for their intentions, at least the Lord's Prayer, the Hail Mary, and the Glory Be seven times each, and the Creed. I recommend it to you. There is a large number of souls who have been in purgatory for a long time because no one prays for them.*

*Commentary: only Catholics among Christian faiths acknowledge the existence of a place of expiation, which is called Purgatory. The Blessed Mother states clearly that it exists. It is described as a place of purification so the soul can then advance to Heaven. God shows His love for his creation by giving us a place to expiate all that stands between a soul and the reward of eternal life.*

Another question is asked concerning Fasting: *The best fast is on bread and water. Through fasting and prayer, one can stop wars, one can suspend the laws of nature. Charity cannot replace fasting. Those who are not able to fast, can sometime replace it with prayer, charity, and a confession; but everyone, except the sick, must fast.*

## July 24, 1982

Concerning Heaven: *You go to Heaven in full conscience: that which you have now. At the moment of death, you are conscious of the separation of the body and soul. It is false to teach people that you are reborn many times and that you pass to different bodies. One is born only once. The body, drawn from the earth, decomposes after death. It never comes back to life again. Man receives a transfigured body.*

## July 25, 1982

Concerning Hell: *Today, many persons go to Hell. God allows His children to suffer in Hell due to the fact that they have committed grave, unpardonable sins. Those who are in Hell no longer have a chance to know a lot better.*

*Commentary: other answers from Our Lady state that people who commit grave sins live in Hell while here on earth and continue this Hell in eternity. They actually go to Hell because they chose it in life and at the moment of death. More on this in the last chapter.*

Concerning cures: *For the cure of the sick, it is important to say the following prayers: the Creed, and seven times each, The Lord's Prayer, the Hail Mary, and the Glory Be, and to fast on bread and water. It is good to impose one's hands on the sick and to pray. It is good to anoint the sick with Holy oil. All priests do not have the gift of heal-*

*ing. In order to receive this gift, the priest must pray with persever-*
*ance and believe firmly.*

### August 6, 1982

Concerning Confession: *One must invite people to go to Confes-*
*sion each month, especially the first Saturday. Here, I have not spoken*
*of it yet. I have invited people to frequent Confession. I will give you*
*yet some concrete messages for our time. Be patient because the time*
*has not yet come. Do what I have told you. They are numerous who do*
*not observe it. Monthly Confession will be a remedy for the Church in*
*the West* (which includes America). *One must convey this message to*
*the West.*

*Commentary: The Virgin is speaking about North America, South*
*America and most of Europe, when she speaks of the west.*

That night, after the apparition, two luminary signs in the form
of rays of light were displayed on the Cross at Krizevac and on the
Church. Ivan and a group of young people had been praying on the
hill of Bijakovici. Before the sign appeared, Mary  said: *Now I am*
*going to give you a sign in order to strengthen your faith.* Many members of the prayer group saw the sign.

### August 18, 1982

Concerning the sick: *Have them believe and pray; I cannot help*
*him who does not pray and does not sacrifice. The sick, just like those*
*who are in good health, must pray and fast for the sick. The more you*
*believe firmly, the more you pray and fast for the same intention, the*
*greater is the grace and the mercy of God.*

Concerning a planned marriage between a Catholic and an Orthodox: *In my eyes and in the sight of God, everything is equal. But*

*for you, it is not the same thing because you are divided. If it is possible, it is better if she were not to marry this man because she will suffer and her children also. She will be able to live and follow only with difficulty, the way of her faith.*

## August 31, 1982

Concerning graces: *I do not dispose all graces. I receive from God what I obtain through prayer. God has placed His complete trust in me. I particularly protect those who have been consecrated to me. The great sign has been granted. It will appear independently of the conversion of the people.*

## September 4, 1982

Concerning praying to the Virgin: *Jesus prefers that you address yourselves directly to Him rather than through an intermediary. In the meantime, if you wish to give yourselves completely to God and if you wish that I be your protector, then confide to me all your intentions, your fasts, and your sacrifices so that I can dispose of them according to the will of God.*

*Commentary: here is solid Catholic Church teaching. The Virgin confirms that we are to pray directly to Jesus, but to also call on her to intercede and dispose of the graces received through prayer. If this message were to reach all people of all faiths, there would be no divisions.*

## January 5, 1983

Ivan, Jakov, Marija, and Vicka relate the following information to Father Tomislav: Marija has received seven secrets; Vicka has received eight; Jakov, Ivanka, and Ivan have received nine; and Mirjana has received all ten. As to how long the apparitions will last, we do not know. Our Lady constantly invites us to prayer, fasting, and conversion and she confirms her promises.

Regarding the time of the sign, its month and year, Ivan says: "It is forecasted."

## January 10, 1983

Mirjana shared with Father Tomislav Vlasic that during the year and a half that she had been receiving apparitions, she had experienced the maternal love and intimacy of Our Lady and questioned her why God could so "mercilessly" send sinners to Hell forever. This was her response: *Men who go to Hell no longer want to receive any benefit from God. They do not repent nor do they cease to revolt and to blaspheme. They make up their mind to live in Hell and do not contemplate leaving it.*

Regarding Purgatory: *In Purgatory there are different levels; the lowest is close to Hell and the highest gradually draws near to Heaven. It is not on All Souls Day, but at Christmas, that the greatest number of souls leave Purgatory. There are in Purgatory souls who pray ardently to God, but for whom no relative or friend prays on earth. God makes them benefit from the prayers of other people. It happens that God permits them to manifest themselves in different ways, close to their relatives on earth, in order to remind men of the existence of Purgatory and to solicit their prayers to come close to God who is just, but good. The majority of people go to Purgatory. Many go to Hell. A small number go directly to Heaven.*

## June 24, 1983

*The sign will come, you must not worry about it. The only thing that I would want to tell you is to be converted. Make that known to all my children as quickly as possible. No pain, no suffering is too great for me in order to save you. I will pray to my Son not to punish the world; but I plead with you, be converted. You cannot imagine what is going to happen nor what the Eternal Father will send to earth. That is why you must be converted! Renounce everything. Do penance. Express my thanks to all my children who have prayed and fasted. I carry all this to my Divine Son in order to obtain an alleviation of His justice against the sins of mankind. I thank the people who have prayed and fasted. Persevere and help me to convert the world.*

## Other messages given in 1983

*Commentary: the messages from this point were given at different times during the last six months of 1983. I list them as they were given to the visionaries by the Blessed Virgin Mary.*

*I know that many will not believe you, and that many who have an impassioned faith will cool off. You remain firm, and motivate people to instant prayer, penance, and conversion. At the end, you will be happier. When you suffer difficulties, and need something, come to me.*

Regarding cures: *I cannot cure. God alone cures. Pray! I will pray with you. Believe firmly. Fast, do penance. I will help you as long as it is in my power to do it. God comes to help everyone. I am not God. I need your sacrifices and your prayers to help me.*

Regarding faith: *Faith cannot be alive without prayer.*

Regarding the (Catholic) Mass: *The Mass is the greatest prayer of God. You will never be able to understand its greatness. That is why you must be perfect and humble at Mass, and you should prepare yourselves there.*

To a priest who asks if it is preferable to pray to Our Lady or to Jesus: *I beseech you, Pray to Jesus! I am His Mother, and I intercede for you with Him. But all prayers go to Jesus. I will help, but everything does not depend solely on me, but also your strength, and the strength of those who pray.*

Regarding souls in Purgatory: *These persons wait for your prayers and your sacrifices.*

Other topics covered during the last months of 1983:

*The most beautiful prayer is the Creed.*

*The most beautiful thing is to believe.*

*All prayers are good, if they are said with faith.*

As if what she had accomplished through the first three years of such personal and revealing daily conversations with the young seers was not enough, the Blessed Virgin Mary added a new development at the beginning of 1984. She would soon start giving a *weekly* message directly for the villagers of Medjugorje primarily through visionary Marija.

The Madonna asked that the parishioners of St. James Church come together at the church for one evening a week so that she could personally direct them in their spiritual life. The priests of the parish chose Thursday evenings for this unbelievable grace. Here is the first message given to the parish on March 1, 1984:

*Dear children! I have chosen this parish in a special way and I wish to lead it. I am guarding it in love and I want everyone to be mine. Thank you for having responded tonight. I wish you always to be with me and my Son in ever greater numbers. I shall speak a message to you every Thursday.*

Thus, from March 1, 1984 through January 8, 1987, Our Lady gave messages to the parish every Thursday.

In early January 1987, there was another change. The Gospa stated she had given just about all that God wished up to this time. However, she would now give a *monthly* message. It was becoming clear that the words from Heaven given at the little village were not meant just for the villagers but for the entire world. Again, they would be given through Marija. Here is the last weekly message given on January 8, 1987:

*Dear children! I desire to thank you for every response to the messages. Especially, dear children, thank you for all the sacrifices and prayers, which you have presented to me. Dear children, I desire to keep on giving you still further messages, only not every Thursday, dear children, but on each 25th day in the month. The time has come when what my Lord desired has been fulfilled. Now I will give you less messages, but I am still with you. Therefore, dear children, I beseech you, listen to my messages and live them, so I can guide you. Dear children, thank you for having responded to my call.*

Here is the first monthly message given on January 25, 1987:

*Dear children! Behold, also today I want to call you to start living a new life as of today. Dear children, I want you to comprehend that God has chosen each one of you, in order to use you in His great plan for the salvation of mankind. You are not able to comprehend how great your role is in God's design. Therefore, dear children, pray so that in prayer you may be able to comprehend what God's plan is in your regard. I am with you in order that you may be able to bring it about in all its fullness. Thank you for having responded to my call.*

Going even further in the grace of teaching her children, The Blessed Virgin Mary continues through her messages to us on the 25th day of each month. She states that was the day Medjugorje actually began with her conversation with the six visionaries. Later she would ask that the anniversary day of June 25 be celebrated in her honor as the Feast Day of the Queen of peace.

The Blessed Virgin has appeared in apparition throughout the centuries as a pure gift of grace to the children of the world. There are several sites closely related to Medjugorje, which prepared the way for the Mother of God to bring it to a conclusion with her appearances in the village.

*Dear children, if you knew how much I love you, you would cry without ceasing!*

> But there are also many things which Jesus did: were every one of them to be written, I suppose that the world itself could not contain the books that would be written.
>
> —John 21:25.

## CHAPTER XV: RELATED APPARITIONS

THREE 20TH century apparition sites appear to be most closely related to Medjugorje. They are La Salette, France, in1846; Fatima, Portugal, which occurred in 1918; and, Kibeho, a tiny, remote village in Rwanda, Africa, where the apparitions began in November 1981, a few months after the start of the Medjugorje appearances.

The tone of the La Salette messages essentially set the stage for the apparitions that would follow. In reading them, one would easily think it applies to the world condition today. Two secret messages were given at La Salette as opposed to the 10 secrets of Medjugorje. They relate directly not only with Medjugorje, but with Fatima and Kibeho.

The Blessed Virgin came only one time to La Salette, on Saturday, September 19, 1846. She appeared to two young children who were serving as shepherds hired by local ranchers. Melanie Calvet, 14, and Maximin Giraud, 11, were checking on the cattle when suddenly they saw a large circle of brilliant light in the ravine below. Running towards it, they watched as it began to open, revealing the figure of a beautiful woman surrounded by light. She was seated, holding her face in her hands as she quietly wept. As they moved nearer, she arose, opened her arms, and began speaking to them in perfect French: *Come to me my children, do not be afraid; I am here to tell you something of great importance.*

The children looked at each other puzzled since they did not clearly understand her words. The woman in the light paused and then changed to their local dialect and repeated the greeting. After identifying herself, she gave Maximin a secret message, which was not to be released until 1858. She then turned to Melanie and gave a long message, also to be kept secret until 1858. However, due to pressures by priests and others, the messages was released in 1851. Here are highlights of the first secret message given to Melanie:

> *Mélanie, I will say something to you which you will not say to anybody: The time of God's wrath has arrived! If, when you say to the people what I have said to you so far, and what I will still ask you to say, if, after that, they do not convert, (if they do not do penance, and they do not cease working on Sunday, and if they continue to blaspheme the Holy Name of God), in a word, if the face of the earth does not change, God will be avenged against the people ungrateful and slave of the demon...My Son will make his power manifest! When these things arrive, the disorder will be complete on the earth, the world will be given up to its impious passions. The pope will be persecuted from all sides, they will shoot at him, they will want to put him to death, but no one will be able to do it, the Vicar of God will triumph again this time.... The priests and the Sisters, and the true servants of my Son will be persecuted, and several will die for the faith of Jesus Christ... After all these will have arrived, many will recognize the hand of God on them, they will convert, and do penance for their sins... A great king will go*

*up on the throne, and will reign a few years. Religion will re-flourish and spread all over the world, and there will be a great abundance, the world, glad not to be lacking nothing, will fall again in its disorders, will give up God, and will be prone to its criminal passions...*

Much of Melanie's secret message pertains directly to France. These excerpts are from the original message; much of it is self-explained; however, the "great king" is believed to be Charles De Gaulle, a devout practicing Catholic who served as president of France from 1959 to 1969. He is credited with returning France to stability and power; yet, the country eventually returned to secularism, where it is today.

The secret given to Maximin was far more revealing. He sent his secret by way of a letter to Pope Pius IX in 1851, doing so a few years before the Virgin's request. It is written in his words as he recalled it. Here is what Maximin wrote to the Pope:

"On September 19, 1846, we saw a beautiful Lady. We never said that this lady was the Blessed Virgin but we always said that it was a beautiful Lady. I do not know if it is the Blessed Virgin or another person. As for me, I believe today that it is the Blessed Virgin. Here is what this Lady said to me:"

*If my people continue, what I will say to you will arrive earlier, if it changes a little, it will be a little later.*

*France has corrupted the universe, one day it will be punished. The faith will die out in France: three quarters of France will not practice religion anymore, or almost no more, the other part will practice it without really practic-*

*ing it. Then, after [that], nations will convert, the faith will
be rekindled everywhere.*

*A great country, now Protestant, in the north of Europe, will be converted; by the support of this country all the
other nations of the world will be converted.*

*Before all that arrives, great disorders will arrive, in
the Church, and everywhere. Then, after* [that], *our Holy
Father the Pope will be persecuted. His successor will be a
pontiff that nobody expects.*

*Then, after* [that], *a great peace will come, but it will
not last a long time. A monster will come to disturb it.*

*All that I tell you here will arrive in the other century,
at the latest in the year two thousand.*[1]

Maximin Giraud

Reaction to the revealing of the two secret messages of La Salette was the same as it is today with Medjugorje; that is, ignorance, disbelief and lack of interest by a majority of the world's population. A close look at the predictions given in the letter written to the Pope shows that only a portion of them have come true. The prediction about France is essentially true today. The part about great disorders seems to be World War II. The "monster" is believed to be Hitler. As to the Protestant country to the north, it is thought to be the United Kingdom.

Regardless, La Salette is included as a site intimately tied to Medjugorje since it was the start of such shocking messages given

---

1 It is thought that Maximin was referring to a year somewhere in the 2000s and not specifically the year 2000.

by the Virgin filled with predictions of future events in the world. Bearing this in mind, it is conceivable to believe that the apparition at La Salette marks the beginning of a *special Marian era* that will run through Medjugorje, thus bringing us to the last apparition of the Blessed Virgin Mary.

A brief look at Kibeho and a more thorough glance at Fatima will show the same relationship in the tone of her warnings and the consequences to the world if ignored. It is very much the same tone of the messages as described to the seers at Medjugorje.

The little village of Kibeho in the African country of Rwanda is obscure and remote—far more than the village of Medjugorje. Like Bosnia-Hercegovina, Rwanda is one of the poorest countries in Africa. Into this similar setting, the Mother of God again comes in apparition to a multitude of visionaries.

What makes the apparitions at Kibeho so closely associated with Medjugorje is that the Virgin announced impending bloodshed on a horrific scale if the people did not listen to her messages. She did the same at Medjugorje, warning of the impending bloody civil war that would come if the people did not listen to her and reconcile with one another. The Serbs, Croats and Muslims of former Yugoslavia did not heed her warning, nor did the majority Hutu tribesmen of Rwanda. Horrific bloodshed, helpless and hopeless refugees and a country nearly destroyed were the fruits at both locations.

The Virgin's warnings issued at Kibeho were deadly accurate. The nation suffered the brutal machete-hacking and club-killing of nearly one million people of the Tutsi tribe at the hands of the rival Hutus. Adding to the horror, Hutu Catholic priests and Protestant ministers joined in the killing.

The Kihebo apparitions began on November 28, 1981, when Alphonsine Mumureke, a sixteen-year-old student in a Catholic school heard a voice calling out "my daughter" to her as she was helping in the dining room. She left the room and saw a beautiful lady in white in the nearby corridor. When Alphonsine asked her who she was, the lady replied, *I am the Mother of the Word.* Alphonsine immediately knew it was the Blessed Virgin Mary.

Alphonsine suddenly felt a strange mixture of indescribable joy and deep fear. Within seconds, she was in a deep state of ecstasy enabling her to see an indescribably beautiful young woman whose skin was an unrecognizable bronze-like color. She was not black or white, just something in-between. The woman wore a seamless dress with a white veil that covered her hair. Her hands were clasped as in prayer and waves of love emanated from her. She began speaking to Alphonsine saying that she wanted to be loved and trusted by the people so that she could lead lost souls to salvation through her Son, Jesus.

Throughout the entire apparition, the young girl was oblivious to her surroundings and classmates. When she came out of the ecstasy, Alphonsine, still prostate on the floor and unable to move, said to the crowd of classmates gathered around and peering down at her, "The Blessed Mother spoke to me." Almost instantly, her classmate began taunting her and accusing her of practicing witchcraft. A young girl named Marie-Claire led the abuse of Alphonsine. Marie-Claire was outgoing, aggressive and very popular with the other girls at the school. She immediately became the unchallenged leader of torment against poor Alphonsine.

To the shock and dismay of not only Marie-Claire but the administrators of the small school, the apparitions to Alphonsine continued daily into the following month, usually occurring on Saturdays. It only made Marie-Claire more determined to expose her as a hoax or someone possessed by evil. Soon, another student, Anathalie, was having the same kind of apparitions beginning in January 1982. She, too, became the target of ridicule by Marie-Claire.

Seventeen-year-old Anathalie could not have been a better choice by the Blessed Virgin to receive such grace. She came from a devout Catholic family and was known for her piety. Her apparitions became as frequent as those of Alphonsine. With two students experiencing such strange, frightening behavior, the school was soon the site of hundreds of curious onlookers who had heard about the apparitions. As the days passed with the apparitions continuing, thousands more came.

Shortly thereafter, a *third* student suddenly started experiencing the same visitations as Alphonsine and Anathalie. Shockingly, it was none other than Marie-Claire, the tormentor of the first two visionaries! She started having apparitions in March 1982. Within days, she was apologizing to the other two.

The former antagonist of Alphonsine and Anathalie agonized over what she had done. Yet, the Virgin filled her with love and gave her important messages. On May 31, 1982, Our Lady said to Marie Claire: ***What I ask of you is repentance. If you recite this chaplet[2],***

---

2 The chaplet is actually another form of the rosary, called the Seven Sorrows of the Blessed Virgin Mary.

*while meditating on it, you will then have the strength to repent. To-day, many people do not know any more how to ask forgiveness. They nail again the Son of God on the Cross. So I wanted to come and recall it to you, especially here in Rwanda, for here I have still found humble people, who are not attached to wealth nor money.*

However, as with Medjugorje, Fatima and La Salette, the warnings of the Blessed Virgin Mary were not just for the country in which she was appearing. She told the young visionary, *When I tell you this, I am not addressing myself strictly to you, child, but I am making this appeal to the world.* Marie-Claire said the Virgin described the world as in revolt against God, stating the world *is on the edge of catastrophe!*

It was not long before huge crowds were streaming into the village and surrounding the little school. It was soon necessary to build a wooden platform for the visionaries to have their visions outside of the school building.

The growing crowds watched the visionaries as they went into spiritual ecstasies that lasted for hours. They witnessed various supernatural phenomena including the dancing of the sun and multicolored displays, the very same phenomena that first occurred at Fatima and later at Medjugorje. Other supernatural signs were stars turning into crosses at night, and heavy rains that came when the visionaries asked the Virgin to bless the crowds. Incredibly, cures were reported to have happened from the rainwater.

During an apparition, the visionaries would go into comatose states for extended periods. As at Fatima and Medjugorje, they were taken by the Blessed Virgin to Heaven, Purgatory, and Hell. They also received secrets that were not to be revealed until told to do so by the Virgin.

The disturbing centerpiece of the Kibeho apparitions came in August 1982. A massive crowd was present, surrounding the large platform. The visionaries were suddenly shown a vision by the Virgin of the savage future awaiting Rwanda if peace was not made between the two tribes that made up the population of the country. Much to their horror, which was evident to the crowd, they saw rivers of blood, burning trees, and countless rows of corpses, many of them headless. All of the visionaries wailed and cried out, begging the Virgin to stop showing them the horror. It would go on for approximately eight hours. The date was August 15, 1982[3] . It had such a terrifying physical effect on the visionaries that some of the onlookers ran away screaming.

At the end of what the Virgin was showing them, the visionaries were told that there would be a "river of blood" if Rwanda did not come back to God. To the horror of the world, it happened. When it came true, other nations stood by and did nothing, including the United States of America.

Bringing the horrendous apparition shown to the visionaries in 1982 to reality, the rampage of killing began in late 1993. A little more than a year later, it had taken over one million lives. Visionary Marie-Clare was one of the slain. Alphonsine's entire family was killed; she herself mercifully escaped. Thousands of dead bodies were thrown into rivers that turned putrid. Thousands of other corpses, many of them decapitated, were left unburied. The stench of death hung over Rwanda. Everything the Blessed Virgin has shown them on that August day had come true,

---

3 This day is the Feast day of the Assumption of the Blessed Virgin Mary, celebrated in the Roman Catholic Church.

Today, Rwanda is mercifully and finally at peace. The apparitions in Kibeho continue to draw huge crowds of pilgrims now coming from many countries. The apparitions, though not as frequent, continue at a random pace with new visionaries.

There were numerous stories of survival and courageous deeds during the genocide. None stands out more than the story of Immaculee Ilibagiza, who lived in a tiny village some distance from Kibeho. When the killing started in her village, she hid in a tiny three-foot by four- foot bathroom with seven other women in the home of a Hutu Protestant minister. These women, which included a child, lived in traumatic fear in this cramped space for 91 consecutive days. The slightest sound could have cost them their lives. The minister risked his own life and those of his family by hiding Tutsis from his fellow Hutu tribesmen, who were obsessively killing all Tutsis, including Immaculee's family. Miraculously, Immaculee and the others survived the ordeal. Only by the grace of God did they go undetected by the killers.

Immaculee would continue the miracle by eventually immigrating to the United States and finding a job at the United Nations in New York City. The courageous young woman then became the author of a book titled *Left To Tell,* published in 2007, which detailed the horror of the genocide and her own story of survival. It became an instant bestseller.

Through the power of faith in God, Immaculee came to forgive the Tutsi neighbors who killed all of her family except for one brother who was away at a private school. She credited the courage to forgive to praying the rosary almost nonstop while confined to the bathroom with the other women. She would become the chronicler of the Kibeho apparitions by writing a book titled, *Our Lady of Kibeho* in the spring of 2011.[4]

After a 20-year investigation, Bishop Augustin Misago of the diocese that includes Kibeho made the pronouncement that the apparitions of the first three visionaries, Alphonsine, Anathalie and Marie-Claire are authentic and recognized as so by the Church. [5]The messages and activities of the other visionaries involved are still under investigation.

The Blessed Virgin first came for the people of the twentieth century in 1917, appearing in the little village of Fatima. As at Medjugorje, her visit took place at a moment of grave crisis. World War I was threatening to end civilization, just as the Virgin had predicted at her apparition site in La Salette, France.

Crises were happening throughout the world. It was a raucous period of tremendous religious, social, and political upheaval; Russia was in chaos, and in Portugal the Christian faith was challenged to the point of extinction by a Marxist-leaning government. Does that sound eerily similar to the world of today?

Into this setting came the Mother of Jesus – again; and again, she came to peasant children, this time, three of them: Lucia, a devout 10-year-old, and her cousins Francisco, age nine, and little seven-year-old Jacinta. Similar to La Salette, the children were tending

---

4 I highly recommend all of Immaculee Ilibagiza's books. They add strong credence to all that the Blessed Mother has given in her messages at Medjugorje and Kibeho.

5 The recognition of an apparition of the Blessed Virgin Mary by the Catholic Church simply states that such an event is "worthy of belief". The faithful are not required to believe an apparition since it does not have direct bearing on salvation for the individual.

sheep in the hills when the Virgin first appeared on the thirteenth day of May 1917. She would appear to them on the thirteenth of the month for the next five months with the final apparition in October.

During the course of the Fatima apparitions, the children were given messages, taught to pray, and, much to their surprise, shown vivid scenes of hell. As happened in the first days of Medjugorje, the visionaries were subjected to ridicule and harassment by the authorities, both civil and religious. No one believed them.

It took a stupendous visible sign to convince the masses that the Mother of Jesus was truly appearing in Fatima. That sign would be the first recorded miracle of the sun, which occurred often in Medjugorje in the early days and continues to happen today. However, it was far more than what is seen in Medjugorje and it lasted much longer. In a dazzling display seen in the midst of a violent rainstorm, the sun seemed to move about the sky, spinning, dancing and appearing to come down from the sky directly at the people. Many believed that it was the end of the world.

A crowd of more than 70,000 people, including skeptics and journalists, witnessed the phenomenon of the sun firsthand. Thousands more saw it in areas surrounding the sight as far away as fifty miles. Amazingly, when it was over, the skies had cleared, the sun shone brightly, and all present were dry and free of the mud that had previously caked their clothing. Believers and unbelievers alike were astonished.

There was more "proof" to come. That additional proof was bold prophecies made by the Madonna. Fatima would become the most prophetic of modern apparitions to occur before Medjugorje. The predictions were part of the single secret given to the young visionaries in contrast to the ten secrets given at Medjugorje. It was believed for many years that there were *three* secrets given to the visionary children. However, it was later learned that it was one secret with three distinct parts.

The first and second parts of the secret given to the Fatima seers contained several elements. First, it referred especially to a frightening vision of hell shown to the visionaries (the first part of the secret). Then, it asked for the formation of a formal devotion to the Immaculate Heart of Mary (the second part). It was in the second part of the secret that Mary also predicted a second world war if people did not convert to God. In addition, it predicted immense damage that Russia would do to humanity by abandoning the Christian faith and embracing Communist totalitarianism. All of the prophecies came true.

After being shown the vision of hell, the children raised their frightened eyes beseechingly to the Virgin who told them, *You saw hell where the souls of poor sinners go. In order to save them, God wishes to establish in the world devotion to my Immaculate Heart. If people do what I ask, many souls will be saved and there will be peace. The war is going to end. But, if people do not stop offending God, another, even worse, will begin in the reign of* (Pope) *Pius XI.*

World War II would be the fulfillment of her prophecy as a consequence of the people not praying as requested. Also fulfilled was the promised sign of the war's proximity: a light seen around the world. That sign occurred in 1939 with the appearance of a strange, worldwide light in the sky, which many reported as resembling an aurora borealis. According to Fatima visionary Lucia in an interview years later, this remarkable celestial event was not an aurora borealis, but a specific phenomenon predicted by the Madonna.

The Virgin proved herself true again on the subject of Russia: *... if people attend to my requests, Russia will be converted and the world will have peace. If not, Russia will spread its errors throughout the world, fomenting wars and persecutions of the Church ...*

The chaos in Russia developed into full revolution, leading to the political development of atheistic Communism and its subsequent spread throughout the world. Ironically, one of the countries infected with the Russian disease of atheism was Yugoslavia, the location of the little village of Medjugorje.

More than seventy years later, the Soviet Union would collapse without a revolution or war. Like toppling dominoes, other Communist countries, including Yugoslavia, followed. No worldly explanation seemed sufficient. Yet, those who believed in the Fatima messages remembered that its fall had been predicted.

The Blessed Virgin then gave visionary Lucia the remainder of the secret of Fatima. This part of the message was not to be revealed by the hierarchy of the Catholic Church until 1960. However, it was decided not to release the final part of the secret out of concern over public reaction to its contents.

On May 13, 2000, the anniversary of the Fatima apparitions, Pope John Paul II unexpectedly announced – not coincidentally on that date – that the so-called third secret of Fatima would be released within days. Followers of the Fatima apparitions were excited. Now, they thought, the world would learn the long-kept mystery of what was to come to the world.

The event came on June 26 – the day after the nineteenth anniversary of the apparitions of Medjugorje. Here is the third part of the Fatima secret in Lucia's own words. It is taken from a written statement she was ordered to write by the bishop of Elyria-Fatima in January 1944.

"After the two parts which I have already explained, at the left of Our Lady and a little above, we saw an Angel with a flaming sword in his left hand; flashing, it gave out flames that looked as though they would set the world on fire; but they died out in contact with the splendor that Our Lady radiated towards him from her right hand.

"Pointing to the earth with his right hand, the Angel cried out in a loud voice: 'Penance! Penance! Penance!' And we saw in an immense light that is God: (something similar to how people appear in a mirror when they pass in front of it) a Bishop dressed in White (we had the impression that it was the Holy Father). Other Bishops, Priests, men and women Religious were going up a steep mountain, at the top of which there was a big Cross of rough-hewn trunks as of a cork-tree with the bark; before reaching there the Holy Father passed through a big city half in ruins and half trembling with halting step, afflicted with pain and sorrow, he prayed for the souls of the corpses he met on his way; having reached the top of the mountain, on his knees at the foot of the big Cross he was killed by a group of soldiers who fired bullets and arrows at him, and in the same way there died one after another the other Bishops, Priests, men and women Religious, and various lay people of different ranks and positions.

"Beneath the two arms of the cross, there were two Angels each with a crystal aspersorium in his hand, in which they gathered up the blood of the Martyrs and with it sprinkled the souls that were making their way to God."

The scene depicted in the third part of the secret is a stark review of the history of the Church during the past century. It is a blunt warning showing where we have been and where we are headed if we do not return to God. In essence, it is a microcosm of what the Blessed Mother has said in her Medjugorje messages.

In a commentary on the entire secret, the head of the Congregation for the Doctrine of Faith of the Catholic Church, Joseph Cardinal Ratzinger, who is Pope Benedict XVI now, states that the "angel with the flaming sword on the left of the Mother of God recalls similar images in the Book of Revelation. This represents the threat of judgment, which looms over the world."

However, Cardinal Ratzinger goes on to point out the most vital point of any and all secrets given in apparition by Mary: "The future is not in fact *unchangeably set,* and the image which the children saw is in no way a film preview of a future *in which nothing can be changed.*"

Then-Cardinal Ratzinger hit the nail directly on the head. The point of any such supernatural event or apparition or locution is to bring about a positive change in the individual soul; it is meant to be a guide for us in the right direction without impeding our gift of free will. Through prayer and fasting, predicted secrets can be changed!

More than sixty years after her startling appearances in Fatima, the Virgin came to Medjugorje. It seemingly appears that all of the earlier apparitions were merely a preparation for the messages of Medjugorje, *The Last Apparition* that heaven is sending through the gracious intercession of the Mother of God. If we have learned well from this preparation, we will believe what she is telling us, transform our lives, and hold on to the hope that is promised.

After nearly 32 years of grace-filled messages given by the Blessed Mother of Jesus Christ at the village of Medjugorje, are the children of God throughout the world going to listen and react as she directs? Will the leaders of the hundreds of religions throughout the world ignore such evident grace because it is thought to be a "Catholic" thing?

Possibly, a positive answer to these questions received an extraordinary boost due to a surprise visit to Medjugorje by one of the most powerful leaders of the Catholic Church in late December 2009. It marked the beginning of a formal acknowledgement of the impact of the apparitions on the world. What transpired during this unexpected visit shocked the villagers and the followers of the apparitions.

*Dear children! Put Sacred Scripture in a visible place in your family and read it. In this way, you will come to know prayer with the heart and your thoughts will be on God. Do not forget that you are passing like a flower in a field, which is visible from afar but disappears in a moment. Little children, leave a sign of goodness and love wherever you pass and God will bless you with an abundance of His blessing. Thank you for having responded to my call.*

—Monthly message given to visionary Marija on January 25, 2007.

## CHAPTER XVI: WHO COULD MAKE THESE THINGS UP?

The Church of Saint James in Medjugorje was packed on an unseasonably warm New Year's Eve in 2009. An electric charge filled the air as the people awaited the start of the Mass. Maybe this would mark the day the Church would at last take serious notice that the Mother of God had been appearing daily in apparition in the little village for more than 29 years.

There was reason for such optimism. All in attendance were singularly focused on the main celebrant of the Mass as he prepared to begin his homily. The celebrant was not one of the Franciscan priests assigned to the parish. Instead, he was a renowned Vatican official, Cardinal Christoff Schönborn from Austria, the noted Archbishop of Vienna

Cardinal Schönborn became the highest-ranking church official to openly visit the village. He is a former student, intimate friend and confidant of Pope Benedict XVI, who, it is all but officially acknowledged, visited Medjugorje *incognito* at least *two* times

195

in the early eighties while serving as head of the Congregation for the Doctrine of the Faith under Pope John Paul II.

Of critical importance, the Cardinal is a member of the same branch of the Church that will eventually rule on the authenticity of the Medjugorje apparitions. He is also regarded by many as "papabile", that is, as a prelate with a significant chance of someday being elected Pope. His resume includes being the primary author of the updated Catechism of the Catholic Church affecting the life and the teaching of the Church around the world. In essence, Cardinal Schönborn has been one of the Church's most influential prelates for more than two decades.

The visit to Medjugorje was not the first interest in Medjugorje for Cardinal Schönborn. He had long followed the events and had invited visionary Marija to the Cathedral in Vienna on September 15, 2009, where she actually had her apparition with the Blessed Virgin. It was an unprecedented act granted by a high-ranking church official. The Cardinal had also frequently spoken publicly about the apparitions, always in a cautious but positive way.

Much to the surprise and joy of the parish, this esteemed Cardinal had come to the village with limited public notice. The excitement created by his presence was elevated by frequent meetings with the Franciscans, the visionaries and many of the visiting pilgrims. However, by his own description, Cardinal Schönborn came unofficially "as a private citizen—just another pilgrim".

Just another pilgrim? Hardly. Cardinal Schönborn is viewed by many as one of the most powerful leaders of the Catholic Church. Now, he was in Medjugorje. After more than 29 years of daily apparitions of the Blessed Virgin Mary, someone from the Vatican was there, in person, in Medjugorje. The crowd could hardly contain itself.

Following the opening liturgy, the Cardinal began his homily. Not far into his prepared text, he paused before exclaiming, "Who could make these things up? Who could invent this thing? Man? No, this is not a human act."

A stir arose from the audience. Was this high-ranking Vatican official actually saying in public he personally believed in the apparitions? As the Cardinal continued, there seemed to be little doubt. He added, "When I see the fruits of Medjugorje back at home, I can only say that the tree is surely good. . . When you look at a place like Medjugorje, you can see a superpower of mercy. . . Many merciful deeds were born here or they were supported here…"

Cardinal Schönborn's comments in Medjugorje would immediately create a sensational and long-awaited positive turn in its often-controversial history. He also celebrated New Year's Eve Mass, adding additional positive comments. After decades of negativity caused primarily by the skepticism and outright disbelief by the two local bishops in office during the ongoing apparitions, it was a confirming moment for millions of believers.

The Cardinal in answer to a frequently asked question added an important statement: Why had the Catholic Church not done more to continue or further investigate the claims of apparitions at Medjugorje? He answered: "I would advise for patience. The Mother of God is so patient with us that for nearly 29 years here, in a very direct way, she is showing her closeness and care for the parish of Medjugorje and numerous pilgrims. We can peacefully wait and have patience! Twenty nine years is a long period of time for us, but not such a long period to our God!"

It was evident that the Cardinal was delighted to be in the village and to have the opportunity to spend quality time with four of the visionaries, Marija, Ivanka, Vicka and Mirjana. Afterwards, he was quoted as stating, "I think that regardless of what will be the ultimate ruling of the Church, one thing is certain: millions of people around the world read these messages and see in them the call of the Mother of God directed to them in their lives. And if the people gather each month to pray, to do penance, to reconcile and to love the Virgin Mary, may we have a better place? That certainly cannot hurt us. Because, in these messages I see a type of school of everyday discipleship of Jesus. Mary just asks us to look at her Son, to hear him, to imitate him. 'Do what he tells you,' were Mary's first words to the people. 'Do what he tells you' is the core of the Medjugorje messages."

Such praise and directness given by Cardinal Schönborn would quickly echo among the followers of Medjugorje throughout the world. It distinctly marked a sharp change in belief in the apparitions among the clergy and the faithful. He would say later that the memories of his meetings with four of the visionaries, Marija, Mirjana, Ivanka and Vicka are carved deep in his heart and he is full of gratitude for the outstanding hospitality in their homes. Adding to the experience, the Cardinal revealed he spent time on pilgrimage as a priest hearing confessions.

The visit by Cardinal Schönborn did not sit well with local bishop Ratko Peric. In mid-January 2010, he posted a statement on the official diocese web site decrying the Cardinal's pilgrimage in December 2009, stating that he did not follow Church precedent by contacting the office of the bishop that he would be in his diocese. "As diocesan bishop," he wrote, "I wish to inform the faithful with this statement that the visit of Cardinal Christoph Schönborn does not imply any recognition of the 'apparitions' related to Medjugorje. I am saddened by the fact that the Cardinal, with his visit, presence, and statements, has contributed to the current suffering of the local church, and even added to it, which does not contribute to the much needed peace and unity."

Cardinal Schönborn immediately replied: "I regret you have the impression that my pilgrimage to Medjugorje did a disservice to peace. Rest assured, that was not my intention."

Despite the bishop's protest, the zenith of the incredible change of perception in the apparitions was reached when Cardinal Schönborn met with Pope Benedict in the second week of January 2010. It was a meeting that had been prearranged, and not because of his pilgrimage to the village. However, the focus of the meeting was quickly altered. According to many Italian media reports, the subject of the Cardinal's visit to Medjugorje was added to the agenda and it soon dominated. This fact was verified by the Cardinal shortly after his Vatican meeting during an interview with a German publication. It was also verified that the Pope did not chastise the Cardinal for his visit to the village, a false rumor reported in Rome newspapers.

While his previous actions concerning Medjugorje indicate a positive personal opinion, it is difficult to conceive that Cardinal Schönborn would have journeyed to Medjugorje without receiving at least tacit "unofficial" approval directly from the Pope. The Vatican enhanced the possibility of that belief with an unexpected announcement. After the Cardinal met with the Pope, a statement was released on March 17, 2010, in which the Vatican formally confirmed that a new 17-member commission would be appointed to immediately begin a thorough investigation of the Medjugorje apparitions. The commission would come under the auspices of the Congregation for the Doctrine of the Faith. It would begin its task shortly thereafter.

The formation of the new Vatican commission to begin a formal investigation of the Medjugorje apparitions was a stunning, unprecedented act by the Church. It constituted the *first time* in Church history whereby the highest office of the Vatican would directly investigate an ongoing apparition site. It is customary for the Church to wait until the reported phenomena apparently concludes its active apparitions before forming a commission to pass judgment on it. Approval or disapproval would come only after a long, exhaustive investigation normally instituted and overseen by the local bishop in charge of the diocese where the apparition(s) took place. However, as stated in earlier chapters, that responsibility was removed from the bishop and assumed by the Yugoslavia Bishop's Conference. It eventually landed directly in the lap of the Vatican.

The very act of forming a new commission under the auspices of the Vatican greatly adds to the premise that it has at least, *officially* recognized what a significant and serious event Medjugorje is on a global scale, giving credibility to the belief that the apparitions are the most important event occurring in the world today. It states without equivocation that it can no longer ignore the impact on the Church and the world itself.

If there was any doubt left about the Vatican's unofficial position on Medjugorje after these events, it was solidly clarified on September 23, 2010. On that date, Cardinal Schönborn hosted Medjugorje visionaries Ivan Dragecivic and Marija Pavlovic-Lunetti at the cathedral in Vienna, with thousands of people in attendance, including many Austrian church officials. It marked the second time that a

Medjugorje visionary had been invited to the Cathedral by the Cardinal. The visionaries opened the activities by spending more than an hour answering questions from the audience. Then, once again, for Marija and the first time for Ivan, they actually had their daily apparition with the Blessed Virgin Mary there in the cathedral.

Cardinal Schönborn brought visionary Ivan back to the Vienna Cathedral in a repeat performance on November 17, 2011, and again on November 25, 2012. By presiding over multiple events in the cathedral that included hosting an active Medjugorje visionary who would again have the daily apparition with the Blessed Virgin in the Cathedral, Cardinal Schönborn added to the positive outlook by the Church on Medjugorje. It set a precedent for the future when all three visionaries still having the daily apparition would have them publicly in front of large crowds during appearances in churches of the Roman Catholic faith.

The new Vatican Commission continued its active investigation into the summer of 2011, having already interrogated visionaries Ivanka and Vicka, as well as Father Jozo Zovko. These interrogations were followed by another with visionary Mirjana a short time later. In 2012, Jakov would be interviewed, as well as an additional session with Ivan. It was then announced by Sarejevo Cardinal Vinko Puljic, a member of the commission that a formal statement would be issued by the commission near the end of 2012 or the early days of 2013. Later announcements stated that it would likely take longer than expected and possibly be made sometime later in 2013.

The outcome of Cardinal Schönborn's visit to Medjugorje and the multitude of positive activities by the commission that followed it, gives indisputable *informal acceptance* of its authenticity by the Catholic Church. How else can it be interpreted when powerful

Church authorities allow such events? Add to this the unwavering informal support and belief in the apparitions by the late Pope John Paul II right up to the time of his death. It would take many pages to list all of the times he made positive reference to Medjugorje, including stating to more than one visiting bishop, that if he were not pope, he would be in Medjugorje hearing confessions! Where it goes from here will be up to the Vatican commission.

We come now to the subject of the secrets of Medjugorje. What do we know about them? How will they affect the world and its people? When will they begin?

Surprisingly, more is known about them than one would expect since they *are* secrets and are not to be revealed until the last apparition has occurred. Yet, out of pure goodness, the Blessed Mother has given hints about them, enough to speculate as to what they will bring to mankind.

Let us see what has been learned about the secret future events that will occur briefly after the last Medjugorje apparition occurs.

*Dear children! Also today I call you to prayer. Little children, pray until prayer becomes a joy for you. Only in this way each of you will discover peace in the heart and your soul will be content. You will feel the need to witness to others the love that you feel in your heart and life. I am with you and intercede before God for all of you. Thank you for having responded to my call.*

—Message given to visionary Marija on July 25, 2003.

> Do not fear what you are about to suffer. Behold, the devil is about to throw some of you into prison, that you may be tested, and for ten days, you will have tribulation. Be faithful unto death, and I will give you the crown of life.
>
> —Revelation 2:10.

## CHAPTER XVII: THE SECRETS

I recall some years ago meeting a young priest in Florida. He was a handsome, charismatic man with a dynamic personality and was a gifted speaker. He was dearly loved by his parishioners because he only preached on subjects that did not offend anyone.

When the priest discovered my involvement in the apparitions at Medjugorje, he quickly let me know he stayed away from such things. In his opinion, praying the rosary and extreme devotion to the Mother of Jesus were out of date habits of worship. Apparitions were probably imaginations of uneducated people. What was needed today to keep the Church vibrant and filled, he said, was more focus on modern social issues and adaptation to progressive modern ways of life.

After giving the young priest a brief version of my experiences with Medjugorje, including the information about the 10 secrets, he asked me with a hint of mild sarcasm, "Why is it that when the Blessed Virgin Mary comes in so-called apparitions there always has to be secrets?"

By this time, it was evident that no attempt to persuade the priest about the purpose of Medjugorje would work. I just shook my head and smiled as I said to him, "I don't know, Father, you'll have to ask God that question since He is the one who sends her."

If I were to answer the same question from a sincere believer who really wanted to know why Mary gives her visionaries secrets concerning the future, I would say it is necessary because without devout spiritual maturity, we *cannot handle the knowledge of what is to come*. I would add that the secrets that are catastrophic *can be altered or lessened* by prayer, fasting and penance. That has happened with the seventh secret, which was catastrophic in nature. Our Lady has confirmed this in her messages repeatedly throughout the nearly 32 years of apparitions. Thus, we can change the *degree* of the predicted catastrophic secrets by putting God in the first place in our life. Yet, Mary also tells us that the final secret will occur because everyone will not convert.

In looking at related apparitions, the secrets given in them also contained warnings. Thus, the secrets given at Medjugorje are in conjunction with the secrets given to the seers of La Salette, Fatima, Garabandal in Spain and Kibeho. All of us have the free will decision to listen and change—or suffer the consequences. Far too often, we have suffered the consequences of death, destruction and darkness.

As we look into the limited information there is about the secrets based on interviews and conversations with the visionaries, as well as the few hints given us by Our Lady of Medjugorje, I repeat a constant theme she gives in her messages: *Do not be afraid.* Holy Scripture backs her admonition by stating the same more than 168 times. God has not sent the Blessed Virgin to earth for her last apparition to scare us into belief, but to assure us of His promise of salvation given on the cross.

It was in early July, just days after the apparitions began when the visionaries first disclosed to the parish priests that the Madonna was giving them secret information concerning the future. According to them, she would progressively reveal to each of them ten future events—secrets—that would occur in the world. They were not to divulge the contents of the secrets to anyone until given permission by the Virgin, not even to the Franciscans or their family members.

The only detail concerning the secrets at the time was that a permanent sign would appear on the Hill of Apparitions on the very spot where the Virgin first began conversation with the visionaries. The sign *was* the third secret. Later, the seers disclosed that the first three secrets were actually warnings to the world that God was real and that the apparitions at Medjugorje were authentic. The secrets in themselves are what will physically change the world. They will bring to reality what we ask for in prayer every time we pray the Our Father prayer: *Thy will be done on earth as it is in Heaven*…and another to the Holy Spirit: *Come, Holy Spirit, come and renew the face of the earth*…

The Virgin has emphasized that attention to the ten secrets should be minimal—that is, know about them, but focus primarily on her messages, which lead to daily conversion. She also said do not wait for the secrets to occur before conversion because it may be too late.

It must be made clear that no one outside of the visionaries knows precisely what the secrets contain. Mirjana, Ivanka and Jakov have received all ten secrets; Marija, Ivan and Vicka have nine of the ten as of the publication of this book. Only the Virgin knows when the last three visionaries will receive the tenth and last secret. Despite this, there are individuals who claim to know all of the secrets based on supposed eschatological studies. They set up web sites or write books to publicize them. These individuals are false prophets, to be sure.

The first three secrets are worldwide warnings given to prove that the apparitions are truly from God. Once all three of them occur, no one will be able to deny the existence of God or that Jesus Christ died on the cross for the salvation of the world. The final opportunity to convert will occur during a brief time after all three have happened. Nothing is publicly known about the fourth, fifth and sixth secrets. Possibly, they relate personally to the visionaries, the Church or the village of Medjugorje. Perhaps there are different secrets for the individual visionaries with these three. However, it has been made clear that the last four secrets are chastisements that will occur in the world—and will unconditionally change it.[1]

It was learned in July 1981, that the secrets would be revealed by a priest chosen by visionary Mirjana. She chose Father Petar Ljubicic, a Franciscan priest who was at one time stationed in Medjugorje but then reassigned to a place a good distance from the parish. Father Tomislav Vlasic, her spiritual advisor at the time asked her why she chose a priest so far away. Within a matter of days, Father Tomislav was transferred out of the parish and the priest Mirjana had chosen was transferred back to Medjugorje! He would leave again later only to return once more; he is stationed there now.

---

1 The general outline on the secrets listed here is strictly the personal speculation of the author based on what has been revealed through the messages of the Virgin, as well as information gleaned from interviews and stories on the visionaries. No attempt is made to state it is a completely accurate account and no dates of occurrence are included.

In the early months of the apparitions, the Madonna presented Mirjana a strange parchment that contained all ten secrets written in an unknown language. The parchment was neither cloth nor paper, but of a material unknown on earth. It could be balled and wrinkled but not torn. All of the secrets are written on this parchment in an unknown language. Of course, Mirjana knows all of the secrets including the day and date of each one. The same is true with Ivanka and Jakov.

Ten days before the first secret is to be revealed, Father Petar will be given the parchment containing the secrets. He will only be able to read the first one. During the ten days, Father Petar, along with Mirjana, will spend the first seven days in fasting and prayer; three days before the event is to take place, he will announce it to the world by whatever means he chooses. At the proper time, he will be able to see and read the second secret, and then the third, etc., according to the schedule of Heaven. Mirjana has stated that Father Petar does not have the right to choose whether to say or not to say what each secret is. He accepted this mission and he has to fulfill it according to God's Will.

A closer look at the first three secrets/warnings gives enough information to lead one to seek conversion as quickly as possible. I include some speculation and state beforehand that the speculation is my personal belief based on research and analysis of the messages the Virgin has given to the world in these last 31-plus years. That includes all apparitions and prophecies which focus on what is to come from Heaven in the so-called end times. More is known about the third secret, the permanent sign that will be left on the hill, while virtually nothing is known about the second secret. It is this secret which I will venture a more in-depth opinion, as well as the tenth secret.

**The first secret:** It was revealed during the first year of the apparitions by the Blessed Virgin that the first secret, or warning, would be a *major upheaval* somewhere in the world. It is not clear if it is to be a geographical, political or religious upheaval. According to Mirjana, it will last for a little while. It will be visible. She says it is necessary to shake up the world a little. It will make the world pause and think. That is the extent of what we know about this secret.

Mirjana had this to say about the first secret in a recent interview: "I now know about things that are not particularly pleasant," she said. "I believe that if everyone knew about these same things, each one of these people would be 'shocked' to their senses and would view our world in a completely different light…. If the people saw the first secret, as it was shown to me, all of them would most certainly be shaken enough to take a new and different look at themselves and everything around them."

Thus, the first secret will focus attention on what is happening in Medjugorje, that it is real and that it affects everyone. It will be the beginning of the awakening of those souls apathetic to the existence of God.

**The second secret:** The second secret may actually be the often prophesized "Illumination of the Soul". Throughout the history of recorded apparitions, locutions, and other supernatural spiritual phenomena, there has been a consistent thread of prophecy that describes an interior "illumination" of the soul that will be experienced by every living human being at a designated time. It is also called the illumination of the conscience.

According to the prophesies, the mass illumination of the soul will occur at a time known only to God, and will suddenly permit every living person to see his or her soul *exactly as God sees it.* It will be given through the Holy Spirit. Every sin committed will be visible to each individual soul, no matter how small or how great the sin; every good deed done will be visible, no matter how small or how great the deed. The world will literally stand still for a matter of time as this incomprehensible grace is given to all living souls. It will reveal to everyone that God truly exists and it will be impossible to deny it after this merciful grace.

Ironically, the Illumination seemingly also occurs to an individual *at the moment* of death or near death. Many near death experiences describe the exact same illumination as that prophesied. Many individuals who went through this experience saw clearly in their own judgments thousands of little slights to others by thought, word and deed. These acts toward others appear to have great weight, things we may consider to be trivial offenses. As one woman who experienced near-death put it, she saw how every nice word or action created light that circled the world while each negative one took that light away.

What happens following the Illumination is up to each individual. Those who believe in God will experience great good from it, while those without belief will suffer with the pain of the undeniable truth that God is real. Some will die from the shock of seeing themselves as God sees them. Yet, everyone will have the free will choice to accept or reject God. Unbelievably, there will be those who will still reject Him.

There are many references to the final illumination in the texts of prophecies past and present. The credibility of the Illumination of the Soul comes from a number of supernatural events. It was allegedly foretold to St. Catherine Laboure in 1830 (at Rue du Bac in Paris, France, the place of the Miraculous medal), to St. Faustina Kowalska in the 1930s (Divine Mercy; Kracow, Poland) and to St. Padre Pio of Italy.

There are numerous others throughout the ages and in our modern times. As always, there are running debates between followers of the saints and prophets who have been credited with receiving this prophecy, as to whether it actually occurred to them. It would take far too much space here to verify the stance of the pros and the cons of each saint or prophet concerning this grace.

Looking to an event closer to our present time, the illumination prophecy was given to four young seers of yet another important 20th century apparition of the Blessed Virgin Mary, which occurred in Garabandal, Spain. The Virgin appeared to them many times from 1961-1965. As with the other apparitions related to Medjugorje, Garabandal also has strong ties.

According to the visionaries of Garabandal, within one year of the Illumination (known there as The Warning), a great miracle will occur in the skies over Garabandal involving a permanent sign that will be left to prove the apparitions are from God. The predicted permanent sign there falls directly in line with the sign that will be left on the hill where the Blessed Virgin first appeared. The sign at Garabandal gives credibility to the speculation that the Illumination of the soul may be the second Medjugorje secret by stating that the sign prophesized for Garabandal will occur within one year *after* the Illumination of the soul.

Further corroboration of the Illumination comes from the locutions given to an Italian priest, Don Stefano Gobbi, who received years of inner locutions from the Madonna. His messages began in July 1973 and continued until December 1997. He was the founder of a movement known as the Marian Movement of Priests, which today consists of tens of thousands of priests. Father Gobbi's locution messages strongly mirror the messages of the Blessed Virgin at Medjugorje. The Movement (MMP) has not been condemned or discredited as reported by another book on the Medjugorje apparitions; on the contrary, it is in good standing with the hierarchy of the Catholic Church.

Appropriately, on Pentecost Sunday, June 4, 1995, the Virgin gave this powerful message confirming the illumination: *Tongues of fire will come down upon you all, my poor children, so ensnared and seduced by Satan and by all the evil spirits who, during these years, have attained their greatest triumph, and thus, you will be illuminated by this divine light, and you will see your own selves in the mirror of the truth and the holiness of God. It will be like a judgment in miniature, which will open the door of your heart to receive the great gift of Divine Mercy.*

A great Catholic theologian named Father Reginald Garrigou-Lagrange (1877-1964) once wrote that "at the moment of separation the soul knows itself without medium, on all its merits and demerits. It sees its state without possibility of error, sees all that it has thought, desired, said, and done, both in good and evil." The entire past, he said, is seen "in a glance." That is precisely what the prophecies of an illumination of the soul have stated.

2

Therefore, the possibility that the great gift of mercy, the Holy Spirit grace of the illumination of the soul, is the second secret of Medjugorje only adds to the credibility that these are indeed the last apparitions of the Blessed Virgin Mary on earth. What greater gift could we be given than to know the full truth of God and then be allowed to choose based on our own free will? It gives great hope for those people whose children and other relatives and friends have abandoned belief in God.

**The third secret of Medjugorje:** The early announcement by the visionaries that the Blessed Virgin said a permanent sign would be left on the hill where she first appeared to them, is arguably the most important of the three warnings because it is visual. As stated, it coincides with the sign to be left at Garabandal. In fact, it may be a possibility that some related permanent sign will appear everywhere the Blessed Virgin Mary has been sent in apparition, which would occur at the exact same time as the sign in Medjugorje appears.

Mirjana would say this about the permanent sign: "When the permanent sign appears, unbelievers will run to the hill and pray for forgiveness . . ." As if to confirm this, the Virgin gave her this message: *This sign will be given for the atheists. You faithful already have signs and you have become the sign for the atheists. You faithful must not wait for the sign before you convert: convert soon. This time is a time of grace for you. When the sign comes, it will be too late. As a mother I caution you because I love you. The secrets exist. My children! Nothing is known of these now, but when they are known, it will be too late. Return to prayer, nothing is more important than this. I would like it if the Lord allowed me to reveal some of the secrets to you, but that which He is doing for you is already a Grace which is almost too much.*

A brief description of the permanent sign from what has been revealed points out that it will be seen as something that has never before been seen on earth. It can be seen and photographed, but it cannot be touched. There is no clue as to why it cannot be touched; does it mean that it is composed of light or a mystical ray that one could put a hand through? Does it mean that it is forbidden to touch it? We do not know.

**The fourth-sixth secrets:** Virtually nothing is known about these three secrets other than what was stated earlier in that they may refer only to the individual visionaries or to the Church. Even this cannot be confirmed; there are no clues from the messages of the Virgin or comments by the seers.

**The seventh secret:** This secret is believed to be the first of the chastisements that will begin the changing of the world. We know this because of the report by the Madonna that by prayer, fasting and penance, it has been mitigated. That means it is either greatly lessened or mostly wiped away. This grace was the result of people listening to the messages and attempting to live them. The other chastisements can also be mitigated or lessened, she revealed through Mirjana, but the tenth will occur, because "everyone will not convert."

**The eighth secret:** On November 6, 1982, Mirjana reported that she was frightened upon learning the contents of the eighth secret, another severe chastisement. She prayed to Our Lady for mercy on mankind with great intensity; the Virgin then said to her, *I have* *prayed; the punishment has been softened. Repeated prayers and fasting reduce punishments from God, but it is not possible to avoid entirely the chastisement. Go on the streets of the city, count those who glorify God and those who offend Him. God can no longer endure that.*

Here again, the Madonna informs us that through prayer, fasting and penance, we can lessen the chastisements that are to come; that is, all but the last, which will happen in full because not everyone will accept the grace of illumination.

**The ninth secret:** All that is known is that it is another severe chastisement to the world. As Our Lady stated, with prayer and fasting it can be at least lessened.

**The tenth secret:** As with the second secret, it is a near certainty that the final chastisement, the tenth secret, has been predicted and prophesized by saints and visionaries throughout the centuries. The Blessed Virgin has said at various times in her messages that once all of the secrets occur, the earth will be purified. The tenth secret will bring about the act of purification.

Therefore, it is reasonable to assume with a strong degree of confidence that the final secret of Medjugorje is the *fulfillment* of the often prophesized **Three Days of Darkness**.

This chastisement has been announced by many mystics of the Roman Catholic Church, such as Blessed Anna-Maria Taigi, Blessed Elizabeth Canori-Mora, Rosa-Colomba Asdente, Palma d'Oria, in Italy; Father Nectou, in Belgium; St. Hildegard, in Germany; Pere Lamy, Marie Baourdi, Marie Martel, Marie-Julie Jahenny, in France; and, most noticeably by Saint Padre Pio of Italy. Although the prophets listed here is a selective listing of saints and visionaries, it is not exhaustive; many more mystics have announced it as well.[2] So many confirming prophesies lend the air of truth to belief that it will occur.

It is important to note that the Roman Catholic Church does not oblige the faithful to believe in any particular prophecy as a matter of faith. It is reasonable to accept that prophecies are made even in our times, as we reported concerning the messages given to Father Gobbi. Such thinking is also corroborated in the Gospels by telling us the Holy Spirit will speak to many souls in the end days. Is that not what is happening in the apparitions of the Blessed Virgin Mary at Medjugorje?

Thus, when an identical prophecy has been made by people widely separated by time and geography, we would be foolish indeed *not* to believe that the prophecy can come to pass. Such is the case concerning the Three Days of Darkness.

The three days of final chastisement will begin on a bitterly cold winter night in the Northern hemisphere. The wind will howl and roar and lightning and thunderbolts of an unprecedented magnitude will strike the earth. The whole earth will shake. The moon and the stars will be disturbed and not be seen in a normal way. Then, every demon, every evil spirit will be released from hell and allowed to roam the earth.

Terrifying apparitions will take place. Many will die from sheer fright. Fire will rain forth from the sky; all large cities will be de-

---

2 It is recommended to take the time to look into the lives of each of those listed here who have predicted the Three Days of Darkness or similar events in nature.

stroyed and poisonous gases will fill the air. Cries and lamentations will be heard everywhere. The unbelievers will burn in the open like withered grass. The entire earth will be afflicted; it will look like a huge graveyard.

We are instructed through the prophecies that as soon as we notice the bitterly cold night, we are to go indoors, lock all doors and windows, pull down the blinds, stick adhesive paper on vents and around windows and doors. We are not to answer calls and pleas from outside, which will sound like our relatives, our children and our friends, even though the temptation will be overwhelming to respond.

In order to protect ourselves, we are to light blessed wax candles, which can be obtained by asking a priest to bless any wax candle. Nothing else will burn, but the candles will not be extinguished once lit. Nothing will put them out in the houses of the faithful, but they will not burn in the houses of the godless. Second, we should sprinkle holy water, again, water blessed by a priest, about the house and especially near doors and windows. The devils fear holy water. We are to bless ourselves with it and anoint our five senses with it— eyes, ears, nose, mouth, hands, feet, and forehead.

We should keep on hand a sufficient supply of drinking water and, if possible, some food—but it is possible to live without food for three days. During the purification, we are to kneel down and pray incessantly with outstretched arms, or prostrate on the floor. We should make acts of contrition, faith, hope, and charity. Above all, we are to pray the Rosary and meditate on the Sorrowful mysteries.[3]

Mercifully, some people, especially children, will be taken up to Heaven beforehand to spare them the horror of these days. People caught outdoors will die instantly. Three-quarters of the human race will be exterminated, more men than women. No one will escape the terror of these days.

When all seems lost and hopeless, in the twinkling of an eye the ordeal will be over. The final secret will have run its course. Once again, the sun will rise and shine as in springtime over a purified earth.

The ten secrets are in reality a great merciful grace. They are not about punishment, but about love—holy divine love. They are an affirmation of the teaching of Holy Scripture, a proclamation of the "Good News" of Jesus Christ. The Last Apparition of the Mother of God at Medjugorje is not one of gloom and doom; rather, it is a joyous gathering together of God's children in an eternal embrace.

Let us see how the apparitions of the Blessed Virgin Mary at Medjugorje has changed the world—and how its conclusion will change it forever.

*Dear children, as a mother I implore you to persevere as my apostles. I am praying to my Son to give you Divine wisdom and strength. I am praying that you may discern everything around you according*

---

3 Even though the Rosary is considered a Catholic prayer, it is strongly recommended that people of all faiths learn to pray this powerful prayer before these events occur, invoking the intercession of the Blessed Virgin Mary.

*to God's truth and to strongly resist everything that wants to distance you from my Son. I am praying that you may witness the love of the Heavenly Father according to my Son. My children, great grace has been given to you to be witnesses of God's love. Do not take the given responsibility lightly. Do not sadden my motherly heart. As a mother I desire to rely on my children, on my apostles. Through fasting and prayer you are opening the way for me to pray to my Son for Him to be beside you and for His name to be holy through you. Pray for the shepherds because none of this would be possible without them. Thank you*

—given to Mirjana on November 2, 2012.

> ...and I heard a great voice from the throne saying, "Behold, the dwelling of God is with men. He will dwell with them, and they shall be his people, and God himself will be with them;
>
> —Revelation 21: 3.

## CHAPTER XVIII: THE LAST APPARITION: HOW IT WILL CHANGE THE WORLD

THERE HAS never been an age such as the one we now live in. Never before, has God been so dishonored and disrespected. Never before, have so few prayed to Him.

Everything in our daily life seems to be more important than the presence of God. Apathy of faith is the overriding reason why the Blessed Virgin Mary has been sent to earth at Medjugorje as a prophet for our times. Never has she come as she has at Medjugorje. More than three decades of daily apparitions to six chosen visionaries sets an unprecedented record for a Marian apparition. The conclusion—the very important conclusion—is presumably close. Afterwards, the secrets will occur and the world will never be the same.

The Mother of God continues to appear for the present. She will do everything possible to bring all of her children to full conversion to God before the secrets begin. She has done so for these last 31 years, bringing great change of heart to millions. It is as though she goes before the throne of God and pleads, "Just a little more time..."

Without the overwhelming achievement of the Medjugorje apparitions, the changing of so many hearts to the ways of God may never have occurred. What would have happened if the goal of destroying the apparitions by the government had worked? How did they survive the attack from within by the two bishops? Had either assault been successful, the result may have been greater chastisement upon the world and it may have occurred sooner. Far more souls would have been lost to perdition.

Therefore, before addressing how the end of the apparitions at Medjugorje will change the world, we need to see how they *have* achieved a major degree of success and changed the world for the better.

We begin with the millions of people who have traveled to the village on spiritual pilgrimage—approximately 50 million through 2011. The numbers steadily increased with the longevity of the event. It is estimated that nearly two million souls made the trek in 2012. The predominant majority have returned to their homelands transformed into children of God. They in turn have been responsible for the conversions of millions more by living the messages as best they can. Stemming from the experiences, dozens of books, articles and digital recordings have been written and made about the apparitions. The readers of the books and recordings find conversion and help spread the messages by passing them on to family and friends.

Hundreds of men and women have discovered a vocation to religious life after experiencing the holiness of the daily focus on God brought about by this gift of grace. Charities have originated there at first to assist the refugees from the horrible civil war that took place, and then to accommodate the hapless and the hopeless in the countries from where the pilgrims come. The convert touched by the apparitions wants to do something—anything to serve and try and live the messages.

Medjugorje itself has been transformed from a tiny rural village into a sprawling town that now has just about any and everything that can be purchased in major cities. Earning a living is no longer dependent on crops of tobacco, vineyards and the maintenance of sheep and cattle. Now it comes from catering to the needs of the pilgrims. This has brought a far higher standard of living as villagers have added additional rooms to accommodate more pilgrims and the prices of just about everything have steadily risen.

Souvenir stands are there by the hundreds; huge department and grocery stores supply all that is needed for the new way of modern life. Yet, the holiness and soul of the apparitions remains in a unique triangle that stretches from the original hillside, Podbrdo, to Cross Mountain, Krizevac, to Saint James Church and its surroundings. None of the commercialism can touch this area.

People of all faiths journey to this holy place. There are programs to serve all age groups and special needs. Each year the youth festival sees an enormous increase in the number of young people from throughout the world. Who would have thought that the gathering of more than 80,000 youth would be focused on faith and not hard rock music? Michael O Brien, a rock musician who found conversion at Medjugorje tells those in attendance at his concerts, "Medjugorje is like a huge rock concert—except with the *real* Madonna!

All of this amounts to the spiritual good fruits spawned by Medjugorje; yet, it is just the tip of the iceberg. There is so much more goodness that has come from this super spiritual miracle. It adds to the contention that the appearances and messages of the Madonna at Medjugorje makes it the most important event in the world today. Of course, what is to come has far more to do with that premise.

On the sad side, in the nearly 32 years of coming to earth in apparition at the village, the Mother of Jesus has cried often. She cries because even though so much good has been accomplished, there is still the vast number of souls who know little or nothing about this incredible grace. Among them are many who really do not care, who refuse to accept the grace offered by her Son. She cries because so few listen even after so much has been revealed during this time. She cries because the number of unbelievers is becoming greater and greater. Yet, out of love for them, the Virgin refers to these lost children as *those who have not yet come to know the love of God.*

Mary continues to ask us to pray for the lost souls and reminds us that the messages given to visionary Mirjana on the second of each month are mainly directed at them. She does not want to lose them to the fires of hell. She constantly points out that here is always hope right to the last moment of life.

There was a deeply revealing message given by the Virgin in July 1982, when the question was asked by one of the visionaries regarding someone who has been bad in life and then asks forgiveness at the last moment of life. The Madonna answered: *Whoever has done very much evil during his life can go straight to Heaven if he confesses, is sorry for what he has done, and receives Communion at the end of his life.*

If we fully comprehend this message, we understand our mission, which is to never cease praying for family members and friends.

With God, there is always hope. It is for this reason we are asked to pray with intensity, why we are asked to fast and to do acts of penance in order to save the unbelievers. They have no idea what awaits them. If they could only take a tiny peek at the content of the secrets she has given the visionaries, surely they would convert quickly. God always forgives those who genuinely convert—even at the last moment.

Sadly, there are more important things for the lost children of today than conversion to the ways of God. The god for many of them is the incredible technology and learning that is increasing at quantum speed. Ever developing technology allows us to live longer and the standard of living, at least in the developed world, is higher than it has ever been.

All of this seems to be for the good. We live in a time when all of these advances are there for us. Yet, we ignore the most pressing needs—especially the declining state of our environment. There is total disregard for nature and for that reason, the environment is a mess. Winter seems like summer and summer seems like winter. Pollution is rampant. Our rivers, streams, lakes, ponds, seas and oceans are filled with waste from mega-factories and huge industrial complexes. Individuals add to the problem with no regard for the consequences. Few seem to care. Animals are disappearing at an alarming rate as we progress in building and expanding until there is little land left for their habitat.

Even with the great gifts of knowledge and technology, no one gives God credit for giving them to humanity. Christianity and most faiths that believe in God are declining. The exception is the religion of Islam, which seems intent on destroying itself from within. Secular humanism is growing like a wild weed. Families are shattered by divorce, adultery and addictions. Priests and ministers are destroyed by scandal for sexual improprieties and greed; many are caught up in the liberal lifestyle of the day. They slowly abandon what they were taught as innocent children.

All of this is happening, while the greatest change in our world slowly erodes away our only salvation, which is belief in our living God. That change is the absolute explosion of evil around the world. How else do we explain the expanding addiction of pornography, drugs and alcohol? How is it possible for a civilized world to turn a blind eye to the horror of child porn and slavery?

The global acceptance of legalized abortion stands as the poster child for this reversal. It is the summation of our spiritual failure. We have rejected the greatest gift from God—life. We trade moral law for civil law. Abortion is the holocaust of today as millions of unborn children are killed daily. Words fail to describe the enormity of this horror.

Many of the lost children—those who have not discovered the love of God, see themselves as the intellectual elite. Intellectualism becomes a god whose name is science. They have been successful in their attempt to overturn our traditional Ten Commandments-based Judeo-Christian morality in conjunction with all other God-believing faiths. They are the ones who have redefined good as evil and evil as good. They are the ones who proclaim the God-centered beliefs and traditions embraced by the followers of Jesus as naïve at best and evil at worst. They are the ones Jesus was referring to when He said, **"I Praise you, Father, for you have hidden from the clever and wise what you have revealed to the merest of babes."**[1]

---

1  Matthew 11:25.

With the high tech communications of today there is no way not to consciously be aware of the negative, anti-God changes that are happening in the world. The same is true of the positive God-given evidence of His existence. We have medical miracles, near-death experiences and, of course, the proliferation of supernatural apparitions of the Blessed Virgin Mary over the course of the centuries.

We are left to wonder, how do people reject God when there is so much evidence of His existence? How do they choose hell instead of eternal life? *Why would anyone deliberately choose to go to hell?*

Visionary Vicka was asked during a recent interview why people choose hell rather than belief in God. The visionary answered the question this way: "We all know that there are persons on this earth, who simply don't admit that God exists, even though He helps them. He always tries to nudge them onto the path of holiness. They just say they don't believe, and they deny Him. They deny Him even when it is time to die. They continue to deny Him after they are dead. It is their choice. It is their will that they go to hell. They choose hell."

Vicka was pointing out that people choose where they are to go at the moment of death. When the illumination of the soul occurs in each individual, they immediately have full knowledge of God and of all truths; thus, they *know* where they are to go.

The visionary went on to say, "The more they are against the Will of God, the deeper they enter into the fire, and the deeper they go, the more they rage against Him. When they come out of the fire, they don't have (a) human shape anymore; they are more like grotesque animals, but unlike anything on earth, as if they were never human beings before. They were horrible, ugly, angry! And each was different; no two looked alike. When they came out, they were raging and smashing everything around and hissing and gnashing and screeching." The sight of what the Virgin showed Vicka and little Jakov when she showed them hell was so bad that Jakov refuses to speak of it to this day.

We now come to the most important question: How will the last apparition of the Blessed Virgin Mary at Medjugorje change the world?

We have seen how the apparitions have brought millions to spiritual conversion. The nearly 32 years of good fruits stand as solid evidence of its success. It has been so successful in bringing souls to spiritual conversion, that the Vatican of the Catholic Church has formed a commission to investigate it. This is unprecedented in the modern history of Marian apparitions for a formal commission to be formed and given the task of investigation before the end of the alleged apparitions.

We also know that there are only three visionaries still having the daily apparition and that all of them have nine of the ten secrets. There is enough evidence to give a general perception of what the secrets contain and that it is the beginning of their fulfillment that will ineradicably bring drastic change the world.

Based on what has been speculated about the secrets, there will be time for the hardest unbelievers to convert. It will be made clear during the three warnings, which are the first three secrets. They will leave no doubt that God is real and that Mary has come in apparition for the last time.

Finally, it is certain that the tenth secret, almost assuredly the often-prophesized Three Days of Darkness, will last for a full 72 hours of raging inferno on earth. When it ends, the earth will be completely purified.

So...what does "purification" of the earth mean?

The people who are left alive, approximately 25-30 percent of the global population, will begin the process of rebuilding the world. They will return to the land toiling in planting and harvesting crops, which will be shared by all. There will be no more greed or hoarding of riches. Everyone will live in harmony.

The purification of the world means more than just the cleansing of the waters and the pollution of the air. It means the purification of the soul. no more killing of one another; no more abortion of the gift of life; no more wars. In short, no more mortal sin.

The children of God who survive the purification will live as in ancient days, worshiping and serving God. The land will yield crops as never before. Mutual trust and honesty will be universal. Prosperity will be very great—not in riches of the past, such as gold, silver and the accumulation of land and other material objects, but in the peaceful sharing so that no one is poor in any way.

This is not to say that life after the purification will be a Shangri la. It will be extremely difficult to readjust to a simple life. Skills of survival will have to be learned on the job. Modern conveniences will be gone for the immediate future. Imagine a world with no air travel, no cell phones, no television or movies. Then imagine the pure peace that will take the place of modern technologies. That peace will be the living presence of the only true peace that passes all understanding: *The peace of Jesus Christ that will then dwell on earth with His Children.* His peace will bring a great calm that will last for an extended length of time. It is not the second coming of Jesus; it is the presence of His real peace among his children on a purified world.

We are left with the last of our vital questions: How much longer will the Mother of God appear in apparition at Medjugorje? Are we close to the time when the secrets will begin to happen?

The answer is simple and straightforward. No one knows the exact time when the apparitions will end or when the secrets will begin to occur, with the exception of the three visionaries who have received all ten secrets. Visionary Mirjana, who has been given the responsibility of releasing the secrets through a chosen priest, knows exactly the dates of when each secret will occur. Imagine having to live with that every day.

We can only speculate on when these things will occur based on what is happening around us. As the visionaries tell us repeatedly, we should know about the secrets and ponder them; and then go about living the messages God has allowed the Blessed Virgin Mary to bring to us. By living the messages, all of which are reiteration of the Holy Scriptures, we become the children of God. That applies to all of us regardless of our chosen pathway to holiness. It does not matter if we are Christian or Jew, Catholic or Protestant, Muslim or Hindu. What matters is the sincerity of our belief and trust in a living God.

One last important note: There is no need to worry about the safety or salvation of our loved ones in the face of what is to come. If we truly trust in the unconditional love of God and accept the gift of salvation given by Jesus on the cross, we will pray for their conversion and protection with confidence.

Our Lady of Medjugorje tells us to give our children and our loved ones to her so that she can intercede for them. As always, she is the mother.

Now, you know.

Prepare. Believe in God. Trust Him.

Pray, pray, pray!

*Dear children, with motherly love and motherly patience anew I call you to live according to my Son, to spread His peace and His love, so that, as my apostles, you may accept God's truth with all your heart and pray for the Holy Spirit to guide you. Then you will be able to faithfully serve my Son, and show His love to others with your life. According to the love of my Son and my love, as a mother, I strive to bring all of my strayed children into my motherly embrace and to show them the way of faith. My children, help me in my motherly battle and pray with me that sinners may become aware of their sins and repent sincerely. Pray also for those whom my Son has chosen and consecrated in His name. Thank you.*

—given to Mirjana on December 02, 2012.

## EPILOGUE

## BUT BY THE GRACE OF GOD . . .

The thought has come to mind a thousand times: what would my life be like today if I had not learned of the apparitions of the Blessed Virgin Mary at Medjugorje?

I shudder when I contemplate the answer.

Twenty-seven years later, I am grateful and in awe that this same mother of Jesus Christ literally spoke to my heart and asked me to make the spreading of her messages my life's mission. In the weakest response possible, I promised her I would try. That was the best I could do.

1 first heard about the apparitions of the Blessed Virgin Mary at Medjugorje In October 1985. It was during a Bible study class talking about modern day miracles that I was teaching. My reaction: I did not believe it. Yet, I was interested enough that the belief by some that the Blessed Virgin was appearing in this strange place might make an interesting story for the four weekly newspapers I owned and operated. That was my only interest—write one story and forget it.

I asked the person in our Sunday School class who had told us about Medjugorje if there were any books or articles on the subject that might help me write a story about it. She told me that the person who told her had a video tape that actually showed the visionaries during the time of the apparition. She was sure she could borrow it for me. The next day, I had the video.

From the moment the video began to play, I knew that this was more than just a story for my newspapers. I watched intently from the beginning. I listened to people being interviewed who had come to Medjugorje on pilgrimage. They were all saying how happy and peaceful they felt in the village.

The video then showed the young visionaries at the time of the apparition. They were all in their late teens and early twenties by this time. As they prayed, they suddenly stopped on the same word, fell to their knees in unison and stared at a spot where they and only they could see her. I watched the reaction of the young visionaries and was stunned. I kept thinking to myself, this is incredible; why have I never heard of such a thing as apparitions of the Blessed Virgin Mary?

Then, in a matter of seconds, my life changed.

I thought as I watched the video, this is real. Quickly, that thought was followed with, if this is real—then God is real. Somehow, I knew at that moment the reality of God. I was overwhelmed with a wave of guilt before suddenly feeling that stupendous message in my heart from this same Blessed Virgin Mary. I can still hear the words: ***You are my son, and I am asking you to do my Son's will.***

My life's mission was to sell my businesses at a very good price and spend the rest of my life having fun. Somewhere in all of that, I was going to write the Great American Novel. That all changed instantly. For the past 27 years, telling the world about Medjugorje has been my mission, fulfilling what the Blessed Virgin asked of me.

I never got the chance to write The Great American Novel. Instead, I wrote a book titled *Medjugorje: The Message*, which remains an international best seller, reaching millions of readers.

In early November 2012, I arrived in Medjugorje for my 111th pilgrimage. Once again, the thought entered my mind: where would I be today if the Blessed Virgin Mary had not spoken to my heart? I realized that it really did not matter. I was here again 27 years later. So was the Blessed Mother. She was still bringing to the children of God the same unconditional grace, which began nearly 32 years ago.

May the beautiful Medjugorje apparitions of the Mother of God continue until every possible soul has had the opportunity to respond.

**—Wayne Weible**

# SELECTED BIBLIOGRAPHY

Weible, Wayne. *Medjugorje: The Message*—Orleans, Massachusetts: Paraclete Press, 1989.

_____. *Medjugorje: The Mission*—Orleans, Massachusetts: Paraclete Press, 1994.

_____. *The Final Harvest*—Orleans, Massachusetts: Paraclete Press, 1999.

_____. *Are The Medjugorje Apparitions Authentic?*—New Hope Press, 2008.

Author unlisted. *Words from Heaven.* Birmingham, Alabama: Saint James Publishing, 1990.

Gobbi, Don Stefano. *To the Priests, Our Lady's Beloved Sons*—St. Francis, Maine: Marian Movement of Priests in the United States of America, 1998.

*Ilibagiza, Immaculee.* **Led By Faith**—*New York, NY: Hay House, 2008.*

_____. ***Our Lady of Kibeho***—*Hay House, 2008.*

Mulligan, James, Rev. *Medjugorje: What's Happening?* Orleans, Massachusetts: Paraclete Press, 2011.

Sakota, Marinko, OFM, *Live with the Heart*—Mostar, Bosnia-Hercegovina: Fram Ziral.

Covic-Radojicic, Sabrina. *Meetings with Fra Jozo*—Paris, France: Les Editions Sakramento, 2003.